The Art of
Bernard Ollis

Robert Buratti
with an introduction
by John McDonald

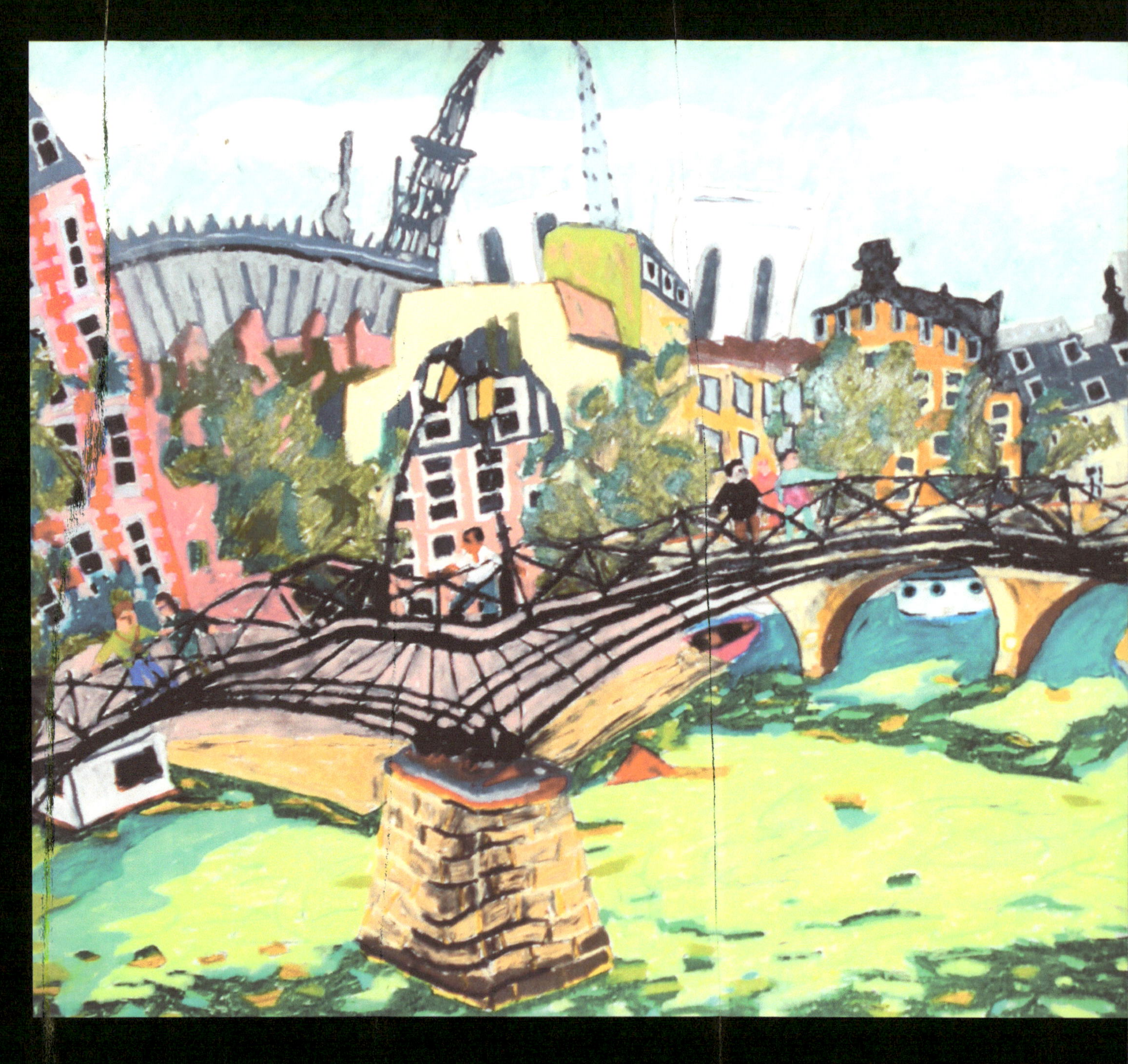

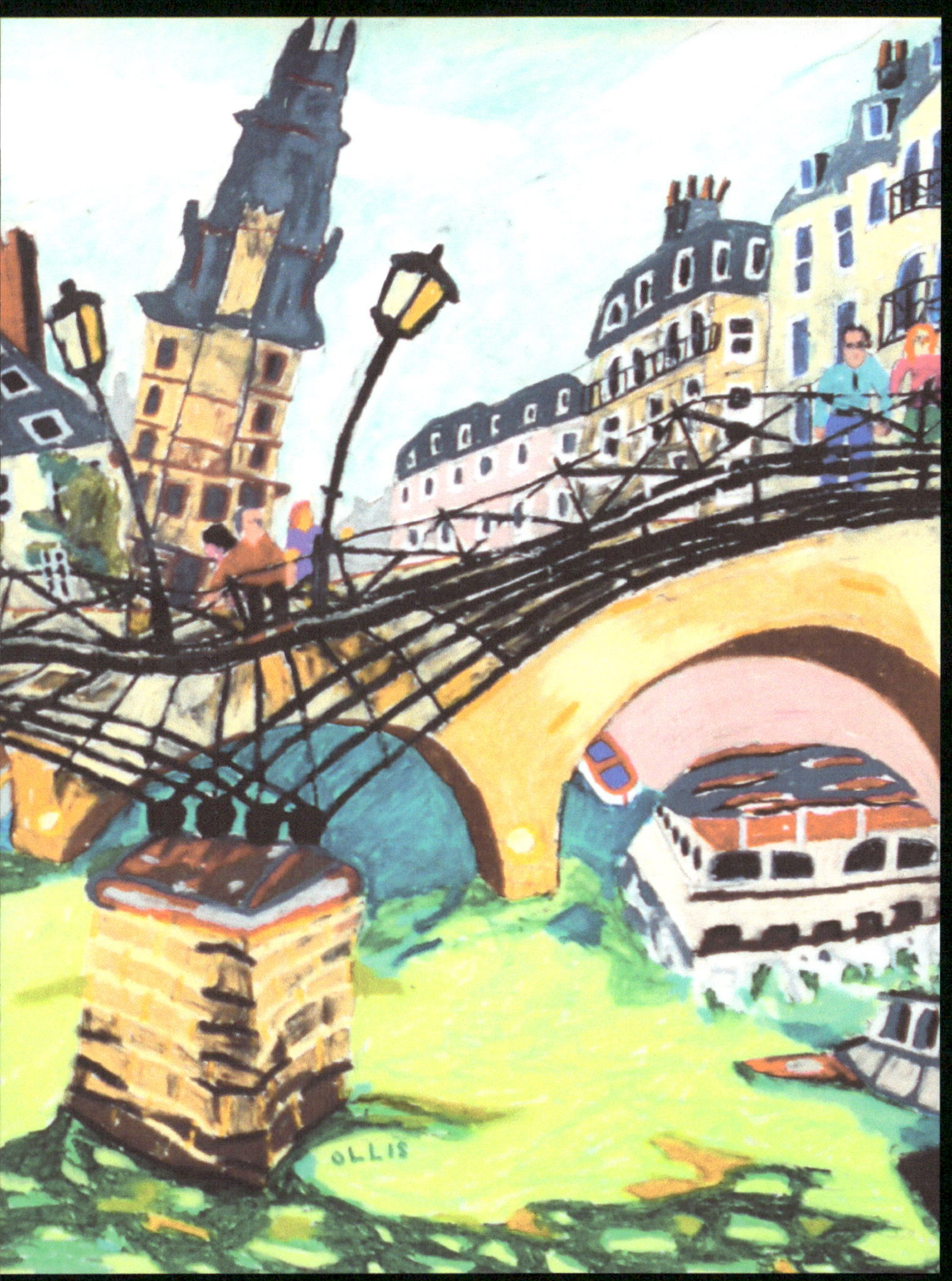

Bernard Berenson argued that paintings should be still and silent, "ineloquent"; but Ollis's pictures are loquacious.

They are not content to sit quietly on the wall as a form of interior decoration, they have an urge to engage with an audience, even if that communication takes the form of a visual puzzle that invites decoding.

John McDonald, 2006

The Pont Des Arts, Paris 2011
Oil pastel on paper
76 x 150cm
Collection of the Artist

The Art of
Bernard Ollis

About the Authors

Robert Buratti

Robert Buratti was born in Sydney, NSW in 1977 and began working in the commercial art world at the age of 18 while completing a Bachelor of Arts at Macquarie University, majoring in English Literature, Linguistics, and Critical and Cultural Theory before moving onto a Master of Art Administration at The College of Fine Arts. He continued to curate exhibitions and work across the commercial art industry in Australia and overseas, before moving to Perth in 2007 and founding the art gallery and arts management company, Buratti Fine Art in 2011 specialising in the promotion, management and sale of many of the country's leading contemporary artists. His previous writing has been published both locally and internationally across a range of subjects and media including Australian Art Review, Artist Profile Magazine and Missoolsidae Korea. Robert is the President of the Friends of the Art Gallery of WA and has lectured at the Perth Concert Hall and the Art Gallery of WA and has been featured on ABC and Foxtel channels.

John McDonald

John McDonald was born in Cessnock, NSW, in 1961, and studied at Sydney University. For over twenty years he has been one of Australia's best-known art critics, writing a weekly column for the Sydney Morning Herald, and contributing to local and international publications. As Head of Australian Art at the National Gallery of Australia in 2000, John was curator of the exhibition, Federation: Australian Art & Society 1901-2001, which toured the country for eighteen months. He has written numerous catalogue essays, and monographs on artists such as David Strachan, Ari Purhonen and Jeffrey Smart. He has also written on films, travel and even cricket. As a lecturer, John has appeared at colleges and public forums throughout Australia, and has taught Art History and Theory at the National Art School, Sydney.

The Art of Bernard Ollis

Published by Buratti Fine Art

ISBN 978-0-9872078-1-4

Photography by Martin Lane

www.buratti.com.au
www.bernardollis.com.au

Contents

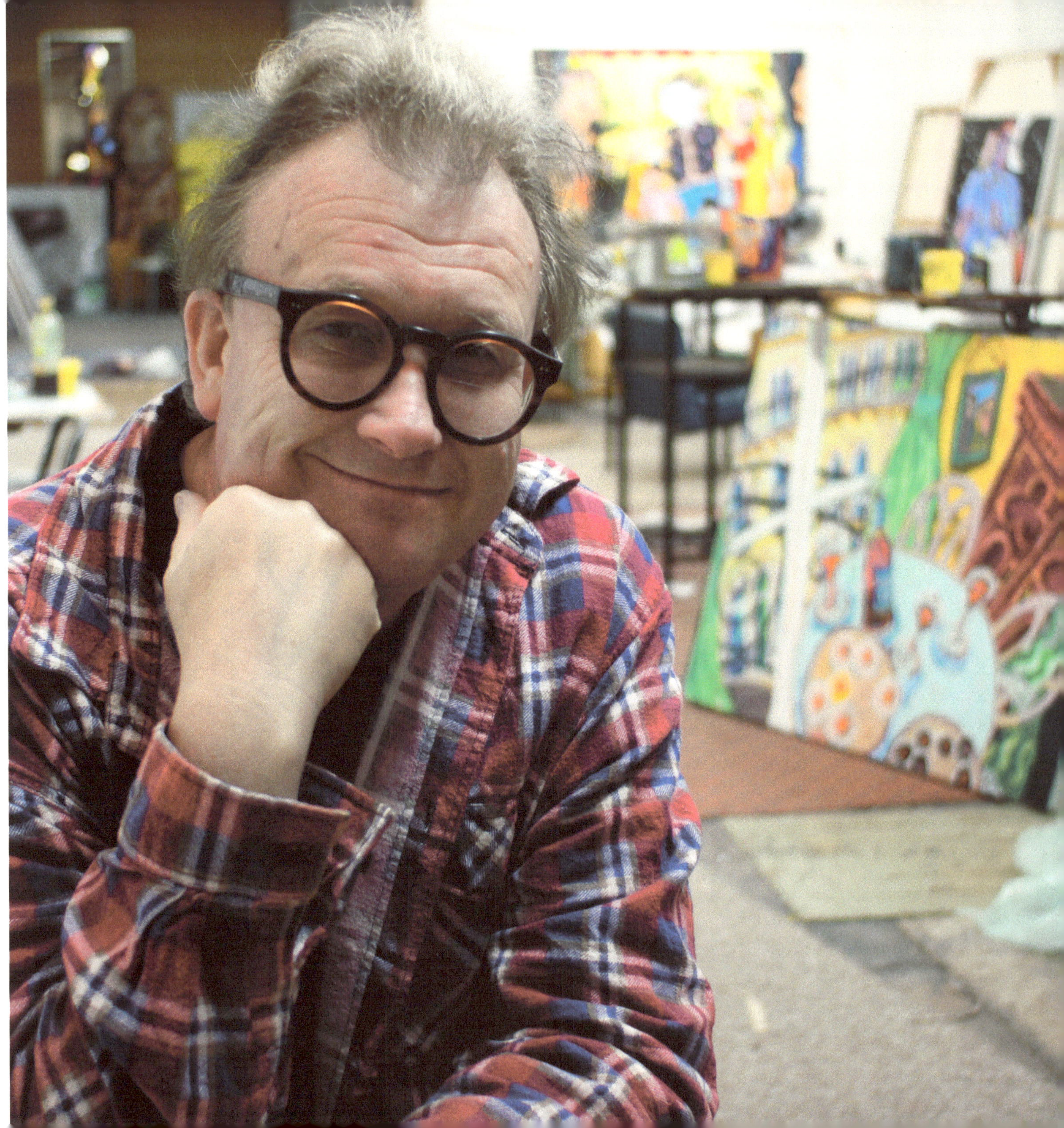

Introduction

Written by John McDonald

Bernard Ollis is one of those painters who elude easy categorization. This is at best a mixed blessing, because art historians love to be able to define an artist as an expressionist, a realist, a surrealist, or some plausible combination. Ollis is a little of each, but ultimately none of the above. He is a figurative painter, but like most established artists is willing to admit that all art is abstract. He is a painter of people, but with none of the angst and pessimism that seem to be standard features of those artists who spend their careers studying the Human Condition. There is a lot of humour in Ollis's work, but none of the smug, all-pervasive irony beloved of the Postmodernists. He is, in short, an awkward proposition, and his paintings revel in a kind of studied awkwardness.

Ollis is a narrative painter, but each picture is nothing more than a fragment. He will begin with a simple setting such as a bedroom, a street, or a patio, and gradually add the dramatis personae and details. A work develops its own momentum, with objects, people or animals multiplying as if by spontaneous generation. While Ollis may begin with a specific idea, by the time the painting is finished it has usually metamorphosed into something quite different.

This is partly a function of Ollis's sheer pleasure in the act of painting. As a former Director of the National Art School, it might be expected that he would have little time to spend in the studio, but he grabs every opportunity with a fierce dedication that few artists can match. Painting is a passion for Ollis, and perhaps a way of escaping the pressures of the workaday world. His pictures, accordingly, are full of fantasy. He creates imaginary scenarios in the manner of a playwright or a film director. Within his own world he can play God. This might mean pumping up the colour, adding a few exotic birds and beasts, or elongating a figure's arms or legs. All of Ollis's paintings have a provisional, slightly vertiginous feeling – spaces are flattened, solid objects seem to waver and tremble, shadows take on a life of their own.

Ollis says he can't remember a time when he wasn't painting, or at least wanting to paint. He was born into a working class family in one of the more prosperous parts of England, near Bath. He worked as a gravedigger, a monumental stone mason, a shop assistant, a baker and a postman, before going to art school. He completed eight years of art education with a three-year stint at the Royal College of Art in London, then set sail for Australia where he has lived ever since. His introduction to the continent, at the age of 25, was a teaching post in Darwin, which provided a crash course in the Australian Way of Life.

Ollis finds that his life experiences keep trickling back into his paintings, by a kind of free association. He will draw a ceiling fan onto a blank canvas, to create a room. His thoughts will drift back to a particular hotel in a foreign country, and he will add a mosquito net and a bedside clock. The view from a window might lead him in another direction. The story keeps changing as new details appear, until finally he decides there is too much going on, and starts to eliminate superfluous elements.

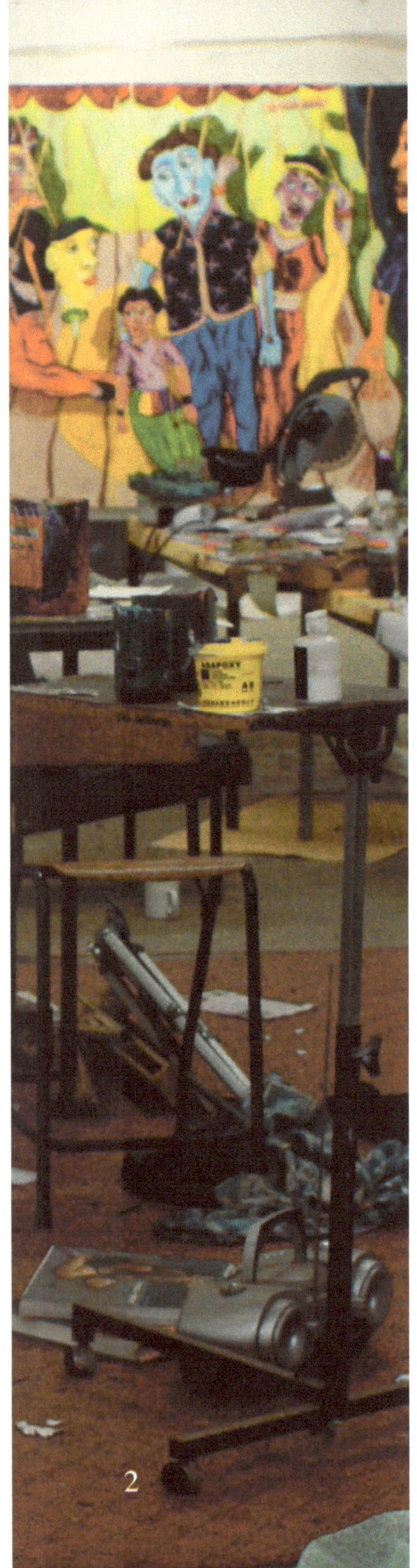

He says he likes the idea of using "the full orchestra, rather than a string quartet," but finds that not every composition is suited to the Wagnerian approach.

Some works, such as a large painting of a ventriloquist and his dummy, have been given a radical reworking to good effect. Coming into the studio late one night, Ollis decided the picture had grown too congested, and blacked out most of the imagery. Afterwards, he added a ring of large birds, which give the work an air of subtle menace – perhaps as a memory of all the savage crows and evil dummies from B-grade horror films, but also because there is something inherently poetic about the idea of displaced speech and frantic flight in a closed, darkened room. Such moments recur at intervals in Ollis's oeuvre. His tones are usually much brighter, the tempo more upbeat. He is happy to describe a lot of his imagery as whimsical, but insists this doesn't mean that he is anything less than deadly serious about the work. If his pictures often resemble stage sets, this is because he is fascinated by the play of semblance and reality that we all enact on a daily basis. In one recent piece he began with two figures, a man and a woman, and gradually began to see the backdrop as a stage set. As he worked, the picture became a vaudeville scene, with the background becoming a painting of a painted backdrop – a double dose of illusion and artifice.

That taste for theatricality is apparent in most of Ollis's paintings, but while his backdrops may appear flat and decorative, he rarely transforms them into stage props. He also avoids obvious instances of melodrama and cliché. Regardless of context, most of his figures wear blank, impassive expressions. He has an explanation for this: "What's happening to them, is happening internally... And hopefully that allows the viewer to identify with them in a more general way." A few years ago, Ollis went through a phase in which almost every one of his characters wore a mask. It was a way of blurring the boundaries between humans and the exotic beasts he loves to paint. In fact, there was no certainty as to what lay behind the disguises. "They might be people, they might be animals, they might be dolls," he says. "When you put on a mask you can get away with murder."

It was also a way of symbolizing the social masks we all wear, and perhaps an homage to James Ensor, one of Ollis's favourite painters. Ensor's early pictures are filled with masks and grotesques, skeletons and dream imagery. Ollis has vivid recollections of the first time he saw Ensor's masterpiece, The Entry of Christ into Brussels in 1889, when it was shown at the Royal Academy in London. In Ensor's painting, Christ appears in a procession, underneath a huge banner proclaiming "Vive la Sociale!" – a celebration of the workers and urban poor who were being let down by the government and the Church.

Ollis might sympathize with Ensor's message - and his extraordinary colours – but he is more likely to show the workers on a day off, rather than marching side-by-side with the Messiah. In one of his recent pictures a brass band in plain uniform trudges down a lonely road by moonlight. One imagines the musicians to be miners or factory workers, making their way to or from some local function. Ollis draws most of his subjects from such ordinary scenes. He shows people in the street or a park, in a cinema or restaurant, perhaps in a hotel room or relaxing at home. He might fill a patio with leaping dogs, birds and snakes, but this doesn't disturb a sleek-looking couple sitting in their easy chairs amid the furore. In this, and other pictures, Ollis cannot resist adding a touch of the extraordinary to an otherwise unexceptional subject. He hopes, always, that some small profundity

"With illustration," he says, "first you have a story about a man walking down a road, and then you set out to capture that scene. I tend to work the other way around, starting with an image or a visual idea, and building a story around it."

In choosing his subjects Ollis tries to avoid anything "too prescriptive", such as a painting with a particular message or moral. On the other hand, he is wary of visual stereotypes: sad and lonely individuals leading lives of quiet desperation, expressions of defiant anger or madness, parables about males and females, youth and old age, wealth and poverty. These elements are all present in Ollis's work, but never in an obvious manner. He likes to set the scene, but hates conclusions. This is also what distinguishes his work from those forms of narrative art that function largely as illustration. "With illustration," he says, "first you have a story about a man walking down a road, and then you set out to capture that scene. I tend to work the other way around, starting with an image or a visual idea, and building a story around it." That story is more like a series of film stills – frozen moments snipped from some larger narrative that neither the viewer nor the artist can ever complete. There is, however, a great deal of sustenance for the imagination. Bernard Berenson argued that paintings should be still and silent, "ineloquent"; but Ollis's pictures are loquacious. They are not content to sit quietly on the wall as a form of interior decoration, they have an urge to engage with an audience, even if that communication takes the form of a visual puzzle that invites decoding.

(left) the studio of Bernard Ollis
(right) The artist working on a rooftop in Florence, Italy

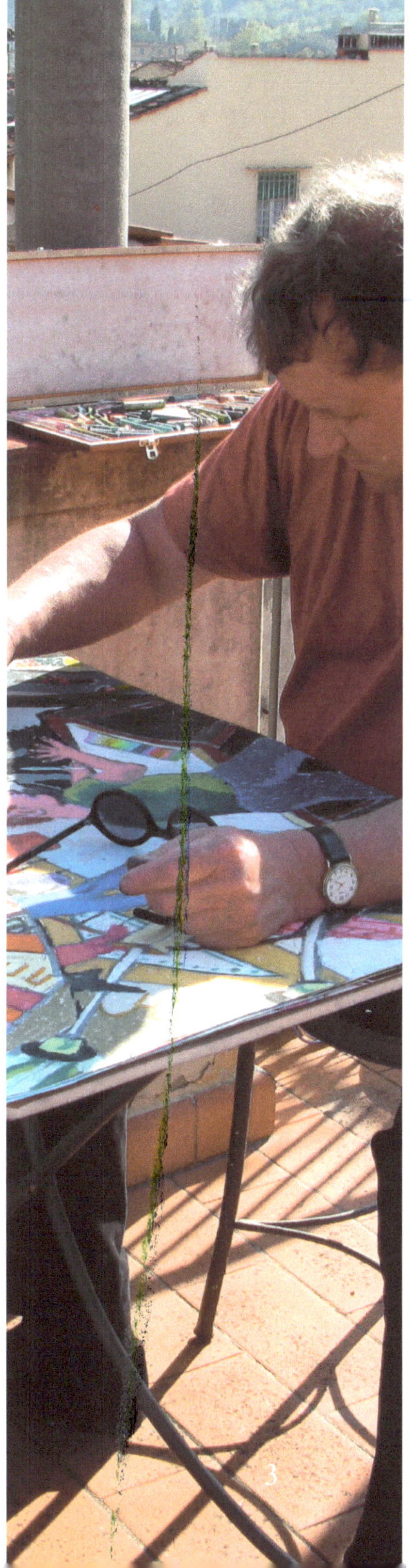

"I understand that the world we live in is one in which people want to absorb the maximum amount of information in the shortest possible time,"

"Painting may be suffering more than most activities, because no-one wants to spend time with things, particularly things that may be challenging or confronting. But painting is a difficult process, and I've always loved the problems it throws up."

Bernard Ollis

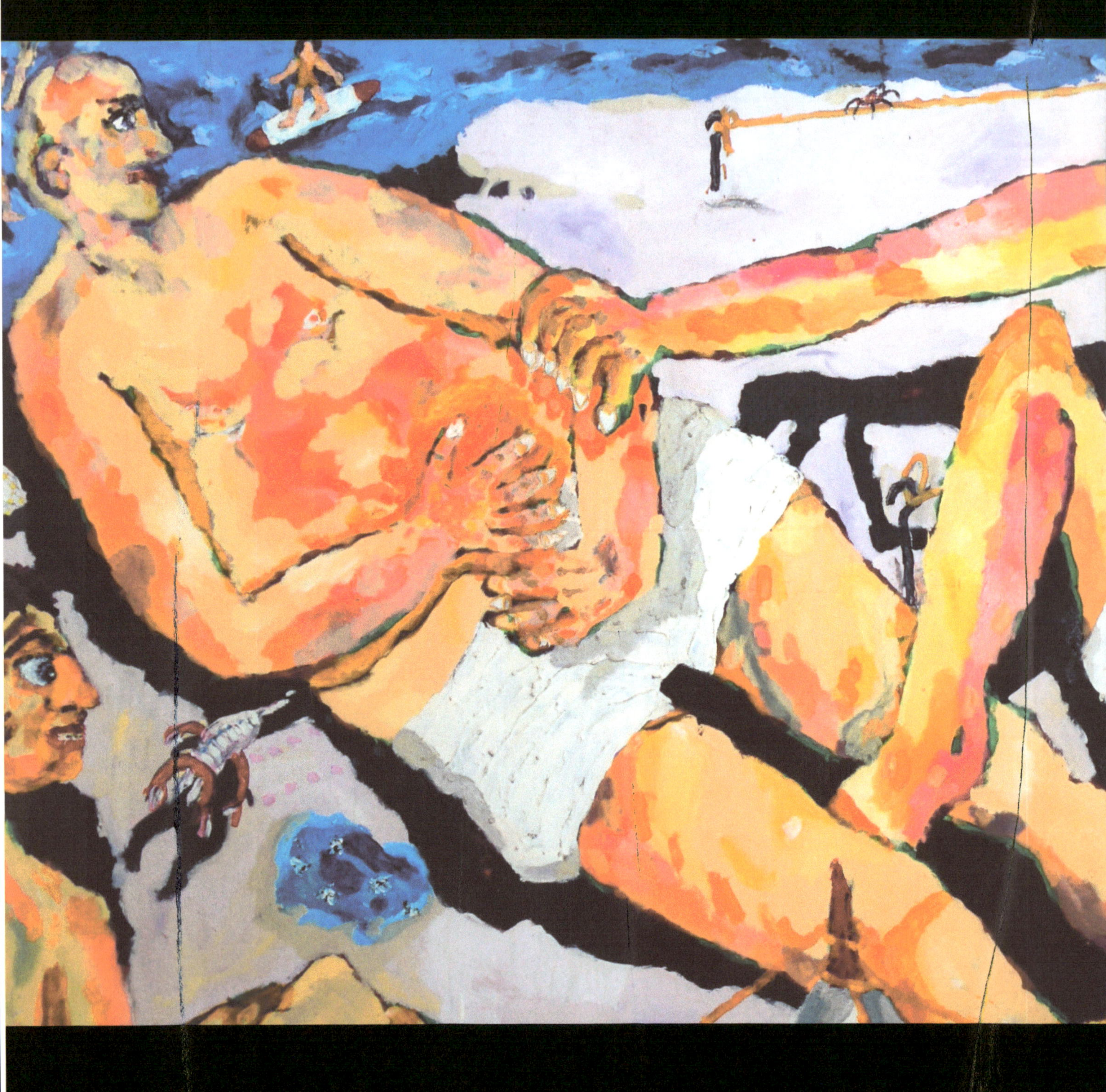

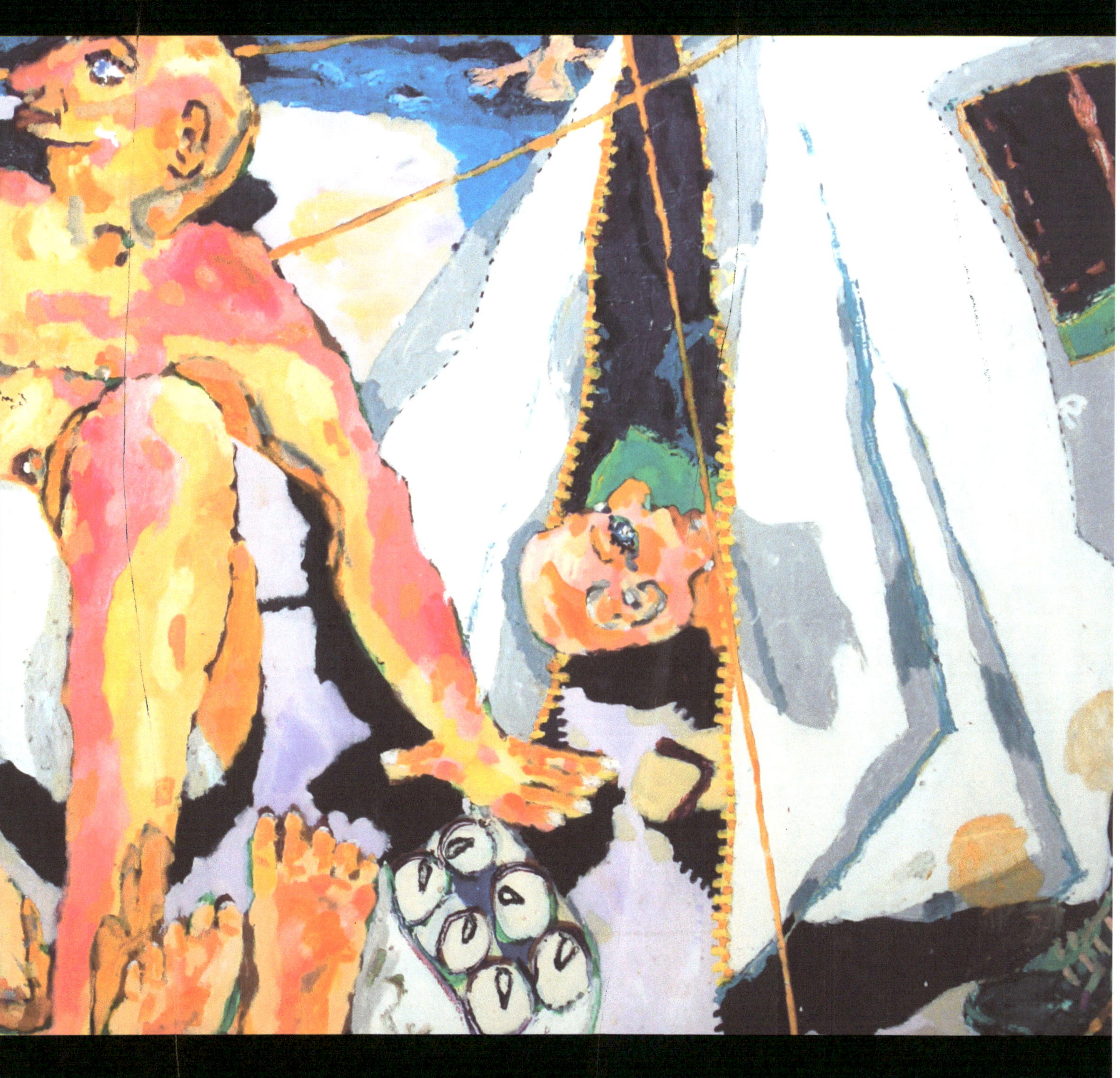

(previous page)

The Bathers
Oil on canvas
172 x 321cm
Collection of the Artist

In the Studio

An interview with the artist

In the Studio

An interview with the artist

I always look forward to visiting the studio of Bernard Ollis. Unlike many artist studios, Ollis' expansive warehouse style space is a continual melee of colour and concept where multiple large scale paintings hang in various stages of creation, alongside ceramics, models and small considered sketches ready to be critiqued and developed into the next manifestation. From the corner, a paper masche skeleton smiles at you, presiding over a plethora of trinkets and keepsakes from decades of globe trotting, and the artist's signature round rimmed glasses sit perched on an easel where exhausted paint tubes are taking a break between rounds.

It seems that there is no "between exhibition" period for Ollis. He is always furiously working on the next painting, and even has a new second studio in Montmartre Paris to use while abroad. I've never walked into Bernard's studio without seeing a new work or idea being born. The studio, like the artist and the work, has a seamless blend of the intellectual and the intuitive.

For an artist who sat at the helm of the National Art School for over ten years, the personal creative practice of Bernard Ollis has remained largely uncharted. Born in Bath, he studied at the Royal College of Art under David Hockney, RB Kitaj and Peter Blake. After moving to Australia in 1976, Ollis began showing across Sydney and Melbourne culminating in over 50 solo exhibitions to date. His unique approach to colour and composition often polarises an audience, and like other Australian painters working with international influences, there is a clear line between those collectors who don't understand Ollis, and those who simply can't get enough of him.

Most recently, the value of his major works have risen considerably, and it seems that his market is on the rise due to a new found popularity with collectors in Australia and the nearby Asian region hungry for significant works which push the conventions of traditional colour and composition.

Since his departure from the National Art School in 2009, Ollis has entered into what will in time be considered an extremely important chapter in his artistic career. I had the pleasure to meet with Bernard Ollis in his Sydney studio in the lead up to his first major Perth solo exhibition.

RB: Sitting here in this huge studio in St. Peters, Sydney, I can't help but wonder how your work must have changed since leaving the National Art School in 2009. How has that separation affected your work?

BO: Well I have always maintained a strong artistic work ethic, even when I was the director of the NAS. I used to say (somewhat romantically perhaps) that making art was at the centre of my universe and the other things like directing an art school, my relationship with my partner Wendy Sharpe, travelling, supporting my children, etc were satellites around that central premise. I worked during that period in short bursts whenever I had an hour or two spare. This is never ideal because you need time in the studio to reflect alongside the physical act of painting. So toward the end of my contract when the pressures and politics of running a big art school started to impinge more and more, I knew it was time to step down. Having an enormous studio only made me feel my absence from it more greatly.

RB: I imagine is was hard to get your momentum on a series of work. Many artists say that is one of the best parts of studying art at university, namely having the ability to focus intently on your practice without interruption. You had a particularly interesting time studying in London at the Royal College of Art as a Masters of Painting candidate during the early 70's. It must have been an incredible period to be there?

BO: Yes, it was pretty special. The course was three years in duration and my studio was in the back of the Victoria and Albert Museum in what was called the mural room. Visiting lecturers included David Hockney, R B Kitaj, Peter Blake, Terry Frost and John Bellany amongst many others, so it was a great place to soak up the atmosphere and learn.

RB: No doubt much of your eventual approach to working came from those amazing influences. I think there are probably three main characteristics in your work which I would like you to expand on. Firstly, colour. It's obviously a major part of your approach, and you've built a reputation as a very recognisable and influential colourist to the next generation of painters. Was a general obsession with colour always part of your approach?

BO: I think colour is one of the great intuitive forces that influence art. Although I went to several major art schools in the UK including the Royal College of Art London and Cardiff College of Art Wales where I learnt the then current mantra of Bauhaus colour theory this only added to things I felt intuitively. At Cardiff I spent months learning about complimentary, harmonic and discordant colour relationships as if it was part of a chemistry lesson, a

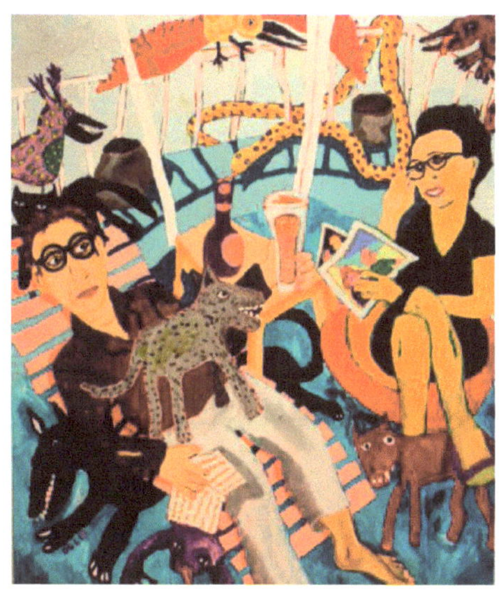

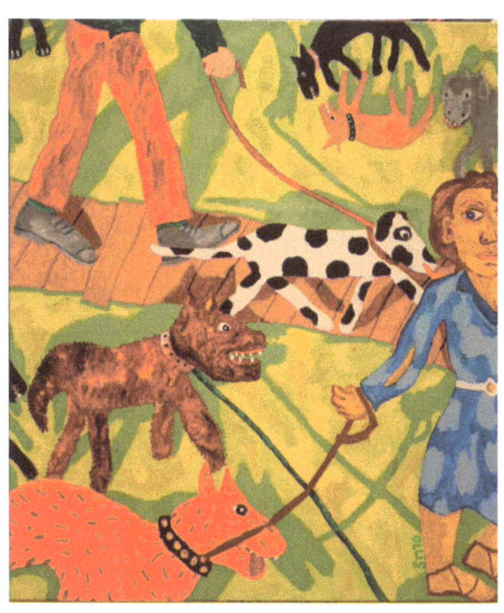

(top to bottom)
Modern Living 2006 oil on canvas 122 x 168cm
Iliych Goes for a Walk, 2006 oil on canvas 122 x 168cm

science that needed to be understood rather than felt, so after all this hands on research I had a better appreciation of Victor Vaserelly or Bridget Riley and how pointillism worked, but the artists I responded to, those that used colour to intensify their subject matter didn't change for me ,they were mainly expressionists with some exceptions, artists like Nolde, Kirschner, Derain, Matisse, Bonnard, Vuillard and a whole lot more.

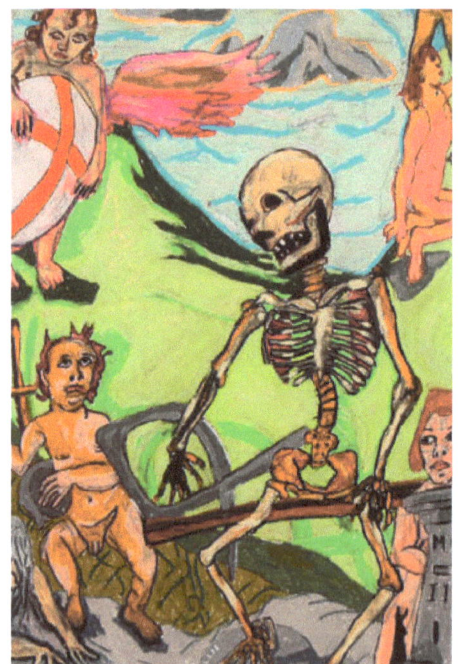

Duomo Ceiling Florence
Oil pastel on paper
80 x 60cm
Private collection, Perth

"I want to step beyond the conventional viewpoint because this for me is dull and obvious and I want to excite and challenge the viewer. I am trying to expand the visual plane so that you can view more than 180 degrees."

In order to do this, I need to twist spaces, elongate shapes, imbue objects with exaggerated proportions and project the viewer into the painting in a way that they would not gain in a conventionally composed work.

RB: The second area I'd like to discuss is your approach to composition. There are very original forces at work here as if twisting or stretching spaces with unusual angles. Can you talk about that aspect of your work and your approach to compositional devices?

BO: I think as I mature as an artist, composition, the way objects and spaces interact on a 2D surface, becomes more and more important for me. I want to step beyond the conventional viewpoint because this for me is dull and obvious and I want to excite and challenge the viewer. I am trying to expand the visual plane so that you can view more than 180 degrees. In order to do this, I need to twist spaces, elongate shapes, imbue objects with exaggerated proportions and project the viewer into the painting in a way that they would not gain in a conventionally composed work.

RB: The last area of discussion is your unusual subject matter. You talk about the Comedie Humaine, and there seems to be a recurring theme of the individual in various stages of flux. It seems that even in works crowded with figures the painting remains the story of a single person within the scene. What role does the individual play within the work?

BO: Yes, the single person may well be me or an extension of my personality: the protagonist. A bit like a male writer often has a central male character in whom the story develops around. I have occasionally painted themes that have no one present, as in my landscapes, but there is evidence of somebody having been there or about to enter. I am interested in narrative, also allegory and symbolism but I never like to be too prescriptive or make any kind of judgement. I want the viewer to engage and step in, as if they had stepped into this arena, it's a bit like writing half a sentence and allowing the viewer to complete it.

RB: I notice there are some recurring concepts of the stage set or arena in which you place the characters. Can you talk about those considerations?

BO: Yes, creating what might be termed a "stage set" has become part of my intuitive process. I can think of many artists who also do this to tell their stories such as Max Beckmann, Edvard Munch, Edward Hopper, and Francis Bacon. They have all used this successfully. I am interested in the human condition and the stage is a wonderful metaphor for stepping into character or transforming identities.

RB: I know that your work to the uninitiated can often appear simple but it seems to me that each work is a very complex inter-relationship of many formal considerations which need to be utterly precise in order to succeed. The more successful compositions are those which have been totally broken down to the most basic forms. Would you agree?

BO: Yes I would like to think so, to get down to the essence of things you often need to distill and eradicate superfluous detail. Matisse for example is the master of this. It looks deceptively simple and art students are notorious for trying to do their versions of a simple line drawing and then of course finding that the deft hand of the master requires enormous skills, knowledge and judgement.

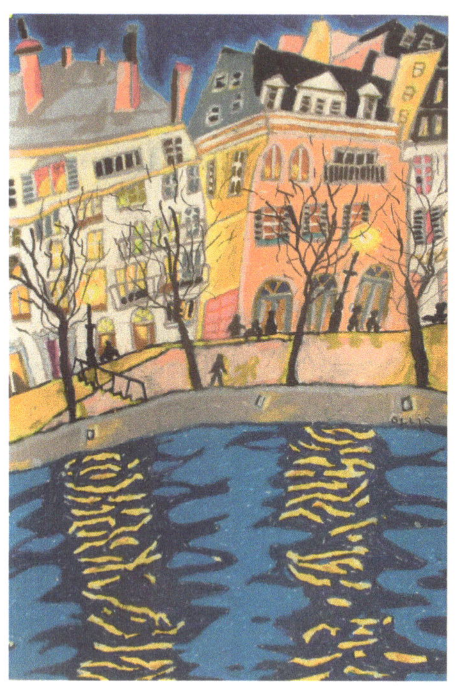

Paris Evening
oil pastel on paper
80 x 60cm
Private collection, Sydney

RB: How do you find your subjects?

BO: They come from everything around me. Every new drawing, print, painting, is for me a new adventure. A journey in which I have no idea of the final result. In that sense its incredibly exciting and frustrating in equal measure. There are good days and bad in the studio and having a good day on the Monday and trying to replicate that modus operandi on the Tuesday never works.

I have never suffered "artist's block", in fact the opposite is true. There are too many ideas floating around in my head. My paintings often have too many things going on in them and I have to be ruthless and sacrifice details for the benefit of the overall.

When students say that they do not know what to paint, I reply, draw what is in front of you, draw your foot, or the crack in the floorboards. Its not critical that Van Gogh chose sunflowers as subject matter, it is what he did with it that counts!

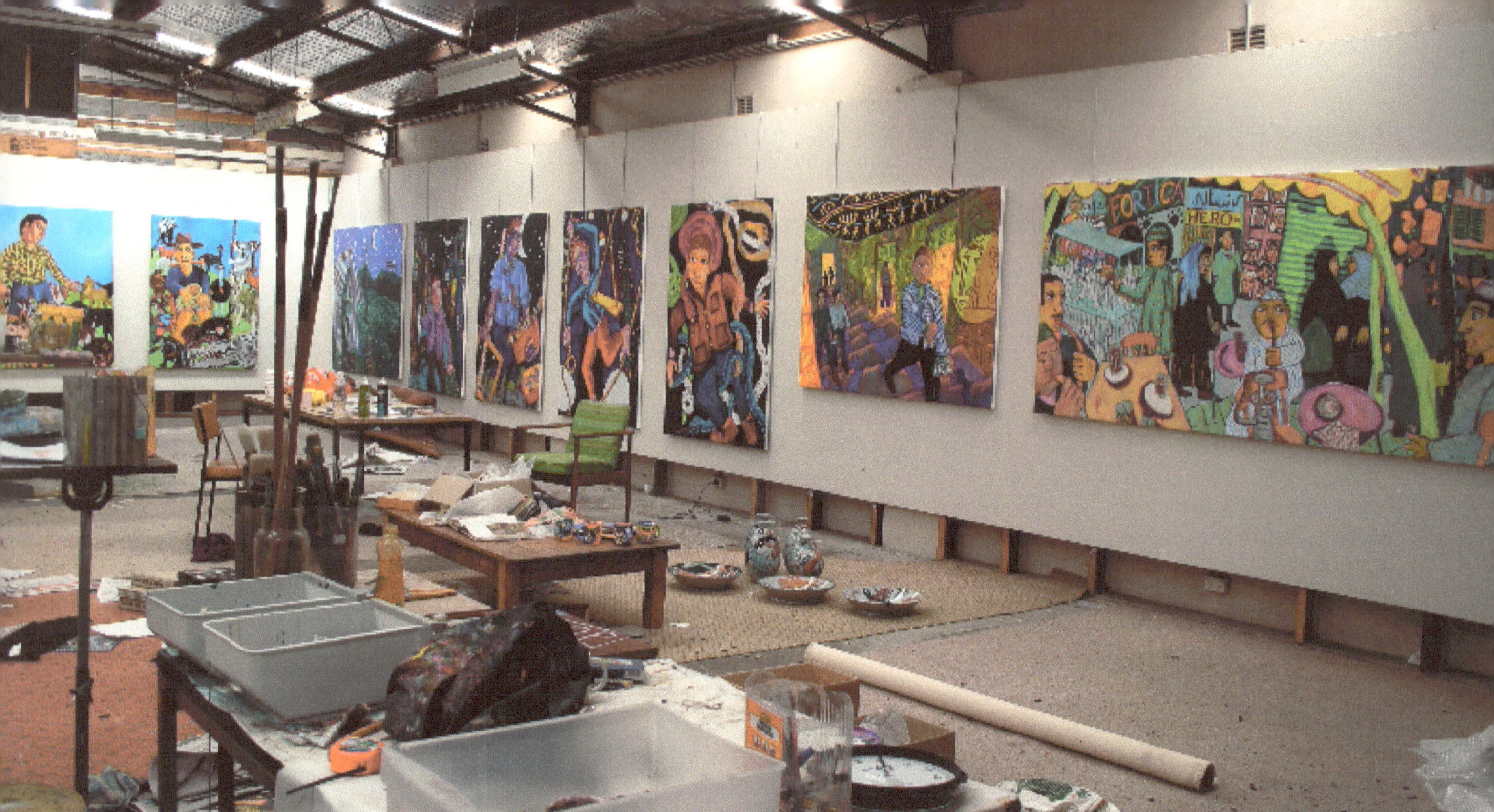

RB: Do you work from imagination or do you produce preparatory sketches or use photographs?

BO: I use all three and I would include making collages and half way through a painting doing more drawings if required, and if all these props are not helping then I might try turning it upside down or reversing the image in a mirror. There are no right ways to begin or end a painting. As a general rule, the more info you have, the more you can overcome problems when they crop up. What I do not want to do is to have a formula or prescription in front of me. The excitement of painting is to keep as many options as possible alive, before bedding it down.

RB: You work on a variety of scales, from paintings over three metres in length to small oil pastels, does your approach differ?

BO: No, it remains the same. There are of course the practical and physical dimensions of working big. It takes longer to apply and make any changes, but conceptually the process doesn't differ.

RB: Travel is a big inspiration for you over the years. What do you look at when travelling ? How important is the act of travelling to your current work?

BO: It is an inspirational activity for any creative person. I find it highly beneficial for my work. I enjoy recording in sketch books ,notepads ,visual diaries the excitement of new terrain .It might be a bus stop in Delhi or an advertising hoarding in Cairo or a row of chimneys in London.

It certainly doesn't have to be glamorous or beautiful, it is about noticing nuances and differences in the way things are put together. Whether that be somebodies clothing ,a toilet seat or a fish market. Trying to decipher how it fits together by describing it in line, tone or colour broadens an

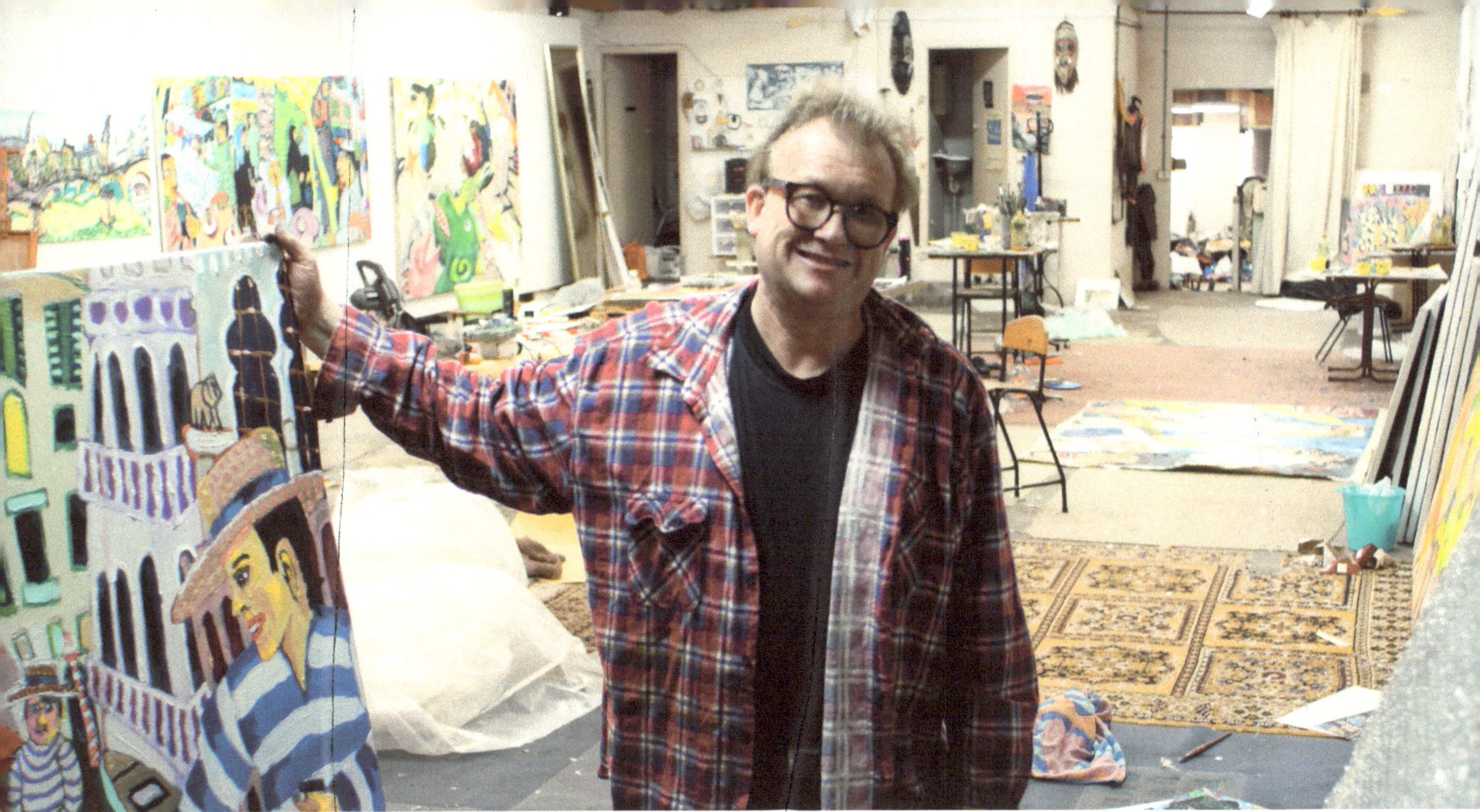

artists language and takes you out of your comfort zone. I think it was that curiosity for the unknown that first led me to Australia, and this remarkable country has never failed to inspire.

RB: You're currently preparing for your next solo exhibition in Perth later this year. After more than 50 solo shows, in Australia and internationally has your preparation and lead up changed over the years?

BO: In many ways the preparation has changed very little. It doesn't daunt me as it once did. Somebody asked me after my first solo Exhibition in Australia (Warehouse Galleries, Melbourne 1978) what it was like, and I described it as akin to taking all my clothes off and running down the main street.

The fear has subsided over the years but it still gives me a buzz to have my work surrounding me on the walls of a gallery, but since I have received everything from accolades to apathy over the years, in the end my challenge is to put together the best show I can. I will always be my harshest critic.

(above)
The interior of Bernard Ollis' Sydney studio.

The Traveller's Eye

The Traveller's Eye

The artistic practice of Bernard Ollis is heavily influenced by the concepts of experience and interaction. As a painter with an insatiable thirst for experiences, he is interested in the urban environment, particularly, in people. His commitment to regular travel is a major driver to the creative process for his recent exhibitions and his regular course for the past five years has spanned Egypt, Italy, France, England, India and Morocco. At the heart, Bernard Ollis is a narrative artist and alongside partner, Wendy Sharpe, has been awarded numerous travelling scholarships and residencies through out his career including studio residencies at Cite Internationale des Arts Paris and the Australian embassy residence Cairo, Egypt as guests of the Australian Ambassador Dr Robert Bowker.

Since the days of antiquity, artists, writers and composers have travelled to foreign countries in search of artistic inspiration. The journey is often as much a spiritual one as a physical one with many artists creating some of their most significant and original work. The effect of new sights, smells and sounds can unlock creative opportunities which otherwise lay dormant under the repetition of usual daily experience. Understanding the aesthetics of a new country can often push an artist to reconsider their own visual language, and also to reconsider their creative decisions and practice within it. In different surroundings, all the senses are heightened with a freshness of vision which is communicated directly to the viewer. Bernard Ollis explains, "Whenever I arrive for the first time in a foreign environment, the best way I can begin to get an understanding of what it looks like, how things are connected, and how people move in and out of it, is to sit and draw it. After a while, what was incomprehensible, starts to make sense."

Since the 17th century, travel was considered essential for budding young artists to understand proper painting and sculpture techniques, and the tradition of the "Grand Tour" is perhaps the best example of the cultural pilgrimage where "a pleasurable stay in Venice and a cautious residence in Rome were essential". Published accounts of personal experiences on the Grand Tour provide illuminating detail and a first-hand perspective of the effect of experiencing new cultures and new ways of seeing. One of the best known accounts is by William Thomas Beckford, whose *Dreams, Waking Thoughts, and Incidents* was a collection of his letters back home in 1780, embellished with stream-of-consciousness associations. Other accounts were recorded by William Coxe, Elizabeth Craven, John Moore, tutor to successive dukes of Hamilton, Samuel Jackson Pratt, and Arthur Young, all of which extolled the virtues of travel and its effect on the creative mind.

In Ollis' travel works, we are sitting with him in an Egyptian cafe among old wooden chairs, sugary coffees and hooker pipes. We can hear the cacophony from the market, the braying of passing donkeys, the sound of motor bikes and the cries of stall holders. The colours of the earth and floating fabrics create new palettes and considerations for an artist to capture and interpret. In another painting, we are standing with the artist on an attic roof in Florence looking over the ancient red tiled roofs to a conglomeration of towers and chimneys. There is a sunset which the artist has never seen before, and the hues of a sky which sits very differently to the deep blue Australian skyline he remembers in inner Sydney. In another we watch the crowds spill through the back streets of Paris while the city hums in the distance and plates and glasses clink in the foreground. Seeing and hearing all of this at once, the artist is challenged to capture not just what he sees, but it essentially what it "feels" like to be there. Ollis' unique approach to his travel inspired work looks quite simple on first viewing, but once the viewer quietens their mind and starts looking and listening deeper, the scene starts to come alive. It's not just a visual diary, but a record of an experience to be relived with each viewing.

(centre strip, left to right)
The artist on various travels 2008 - 2010 | Rajasthan, India | Siena, Italy | Florence, Italy | The White Desert, Egypt
main image: The artist drawing in a cafe in Cairo, Egypt

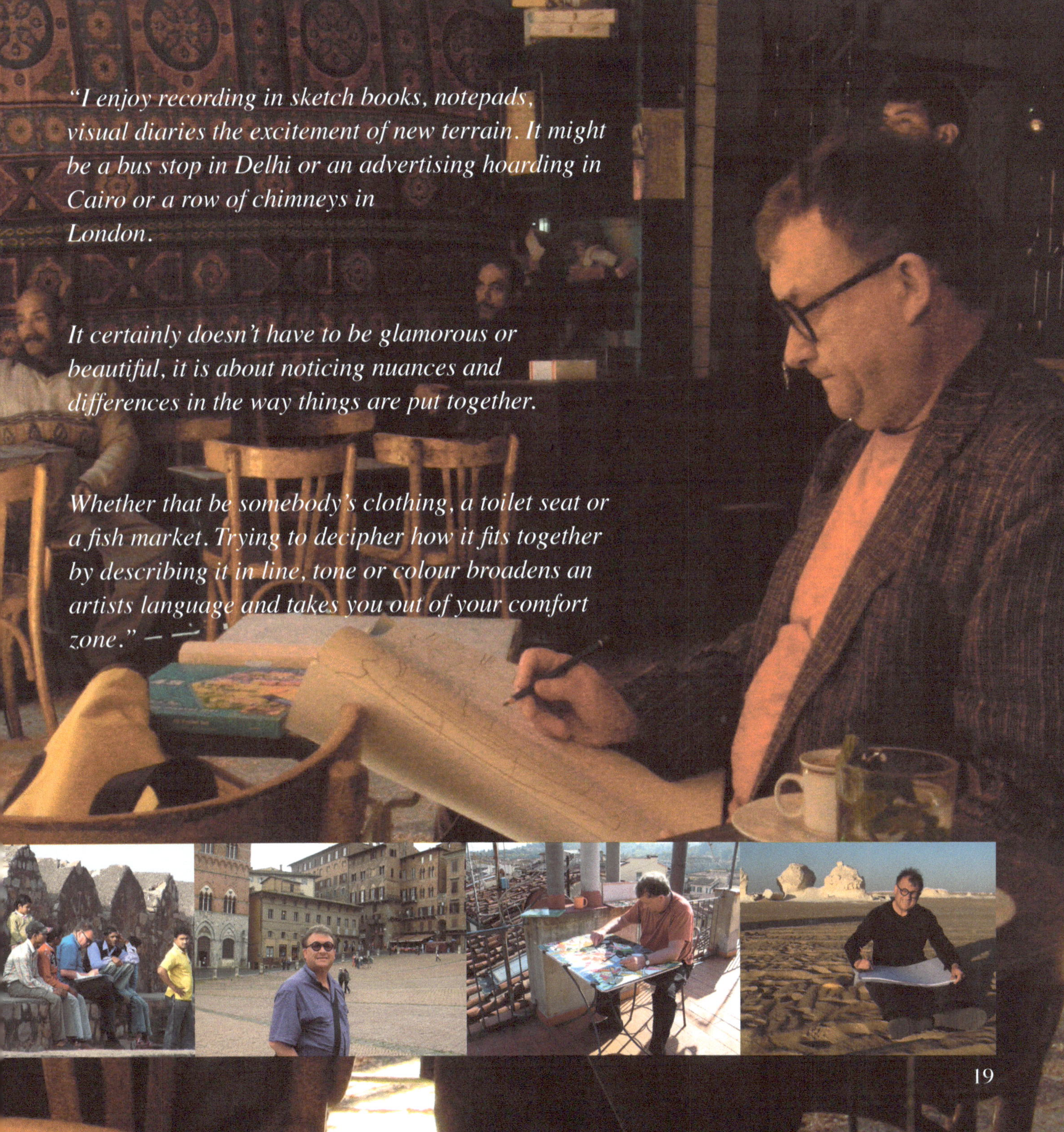

"I enjoy recording in sketch books, notepads, visual diaries the excitement of new terrain. It might be a bus stop in Delhi or an advertising hoarding in Cairo or a row of chimneys in London.

It certainly doesn't have to be glamorous or beautiful, it is about noticing nuances and differences in the way things are put together.

Whether that be somebody's clothing, a toilet seat or a fish market. Trying to decipher how it fits together by describing it in line, tone or colour broadens an artists language and takes you out of your comfort zone."

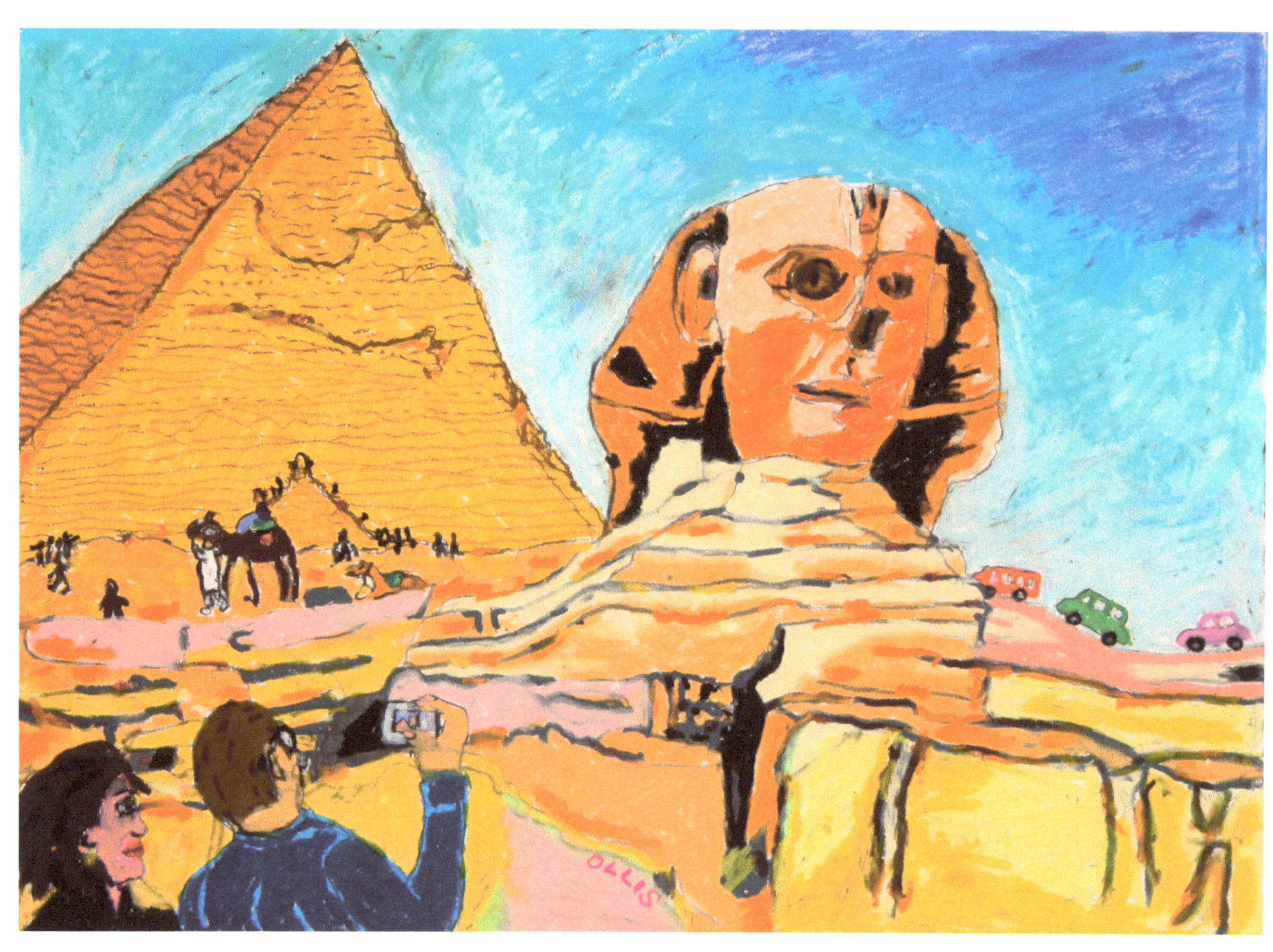

Giza for the Tourist
Oil pastel on paper
42 x 59.4cm
Collection of the Artist

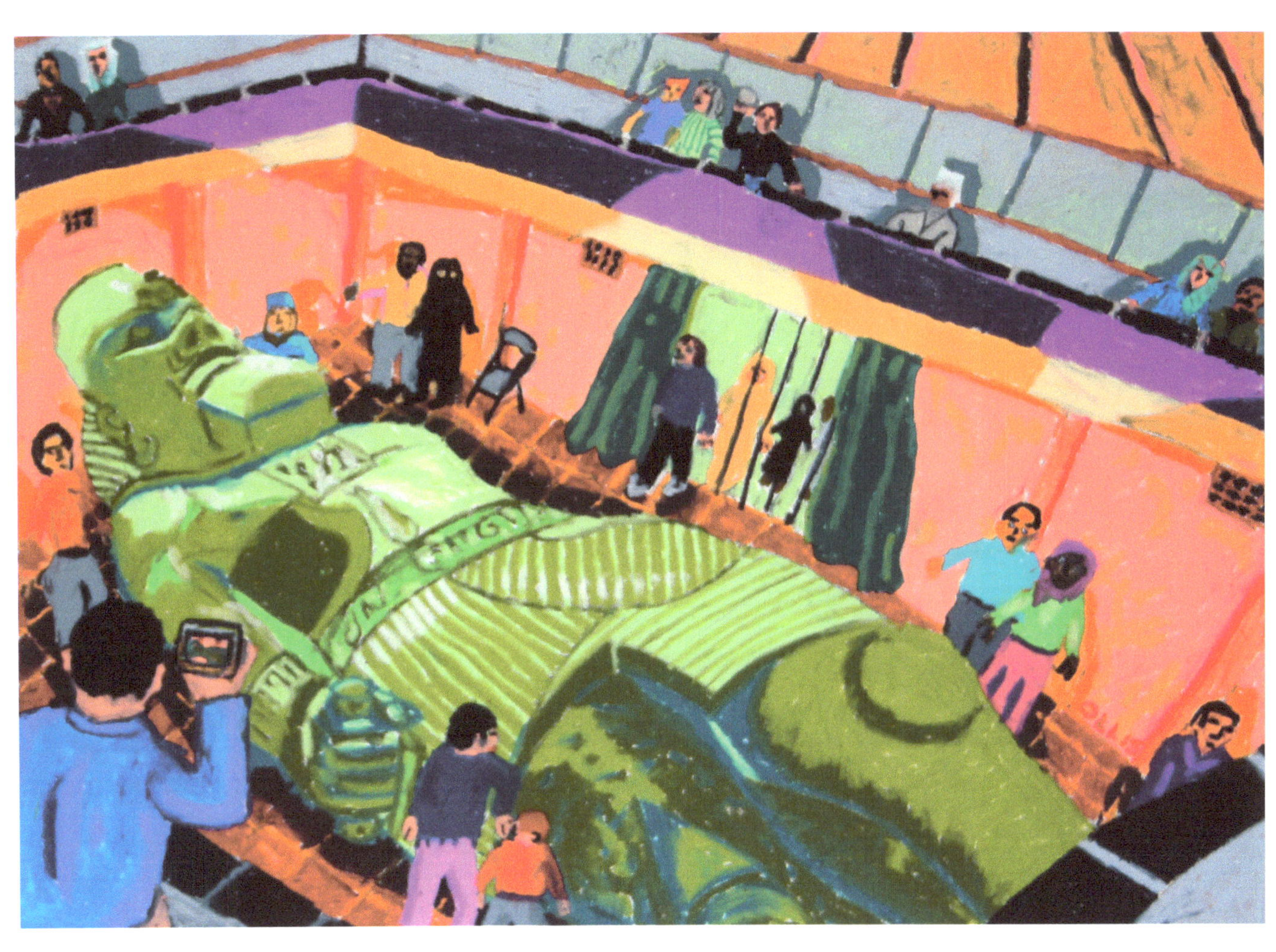

The Collossus of Ramses II
Oil pastel on paper
42 x 59.4cm
Collection of the Artist

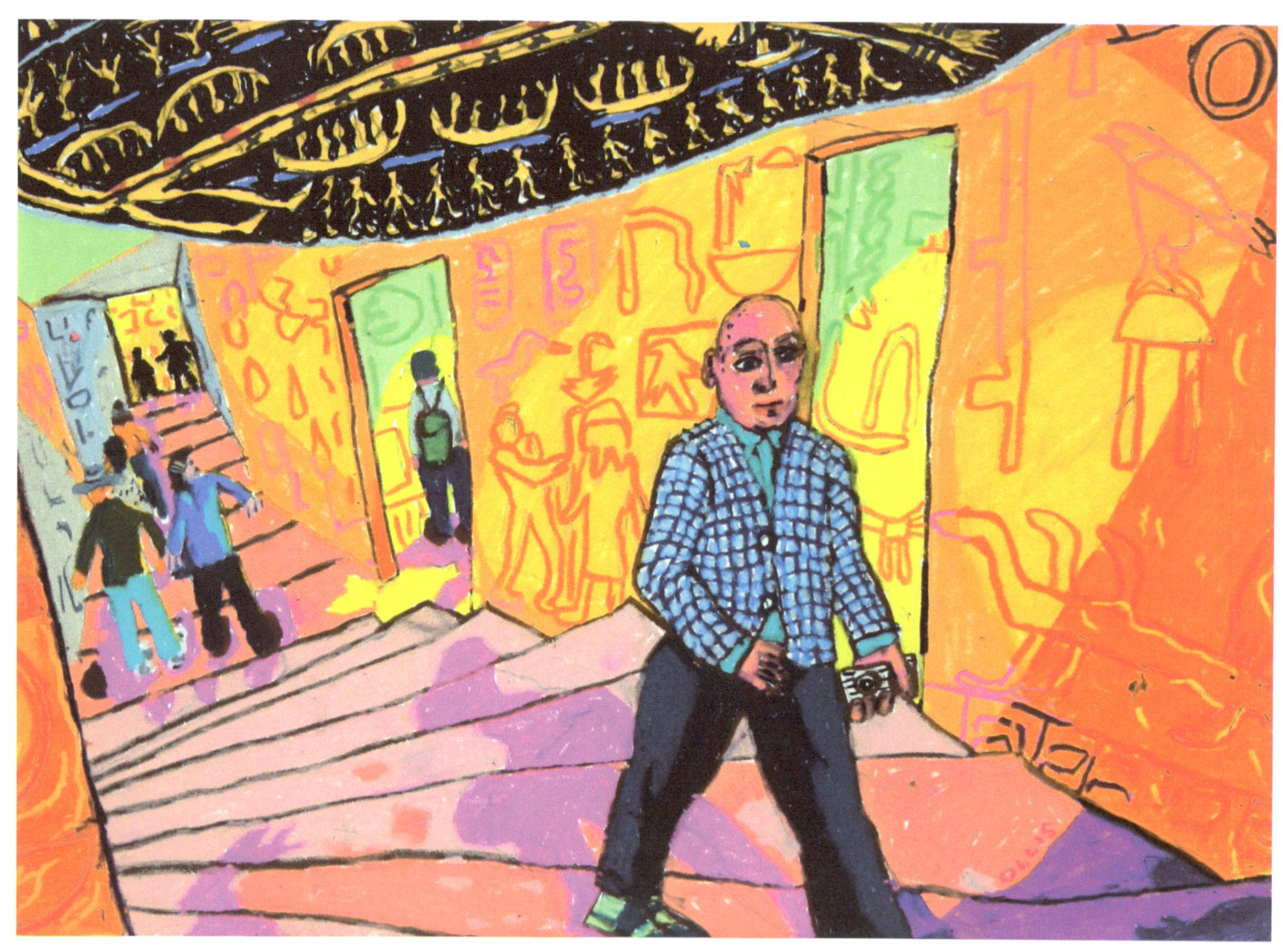

Valley of the Kings
Oil pastel on paper
42 x 59.4cm
Collection of the Artist

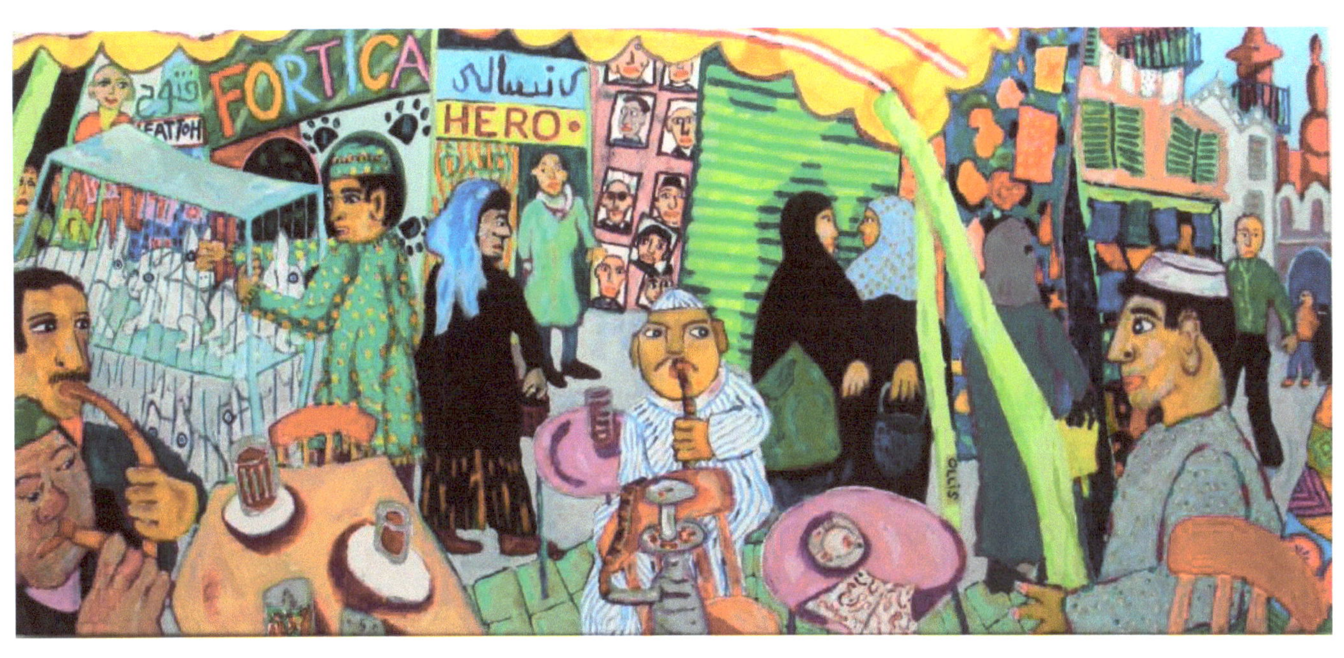

Cairo Market, Khan Al Khalli
Oil on canvas
170 x 300cm
Collection of the Artist

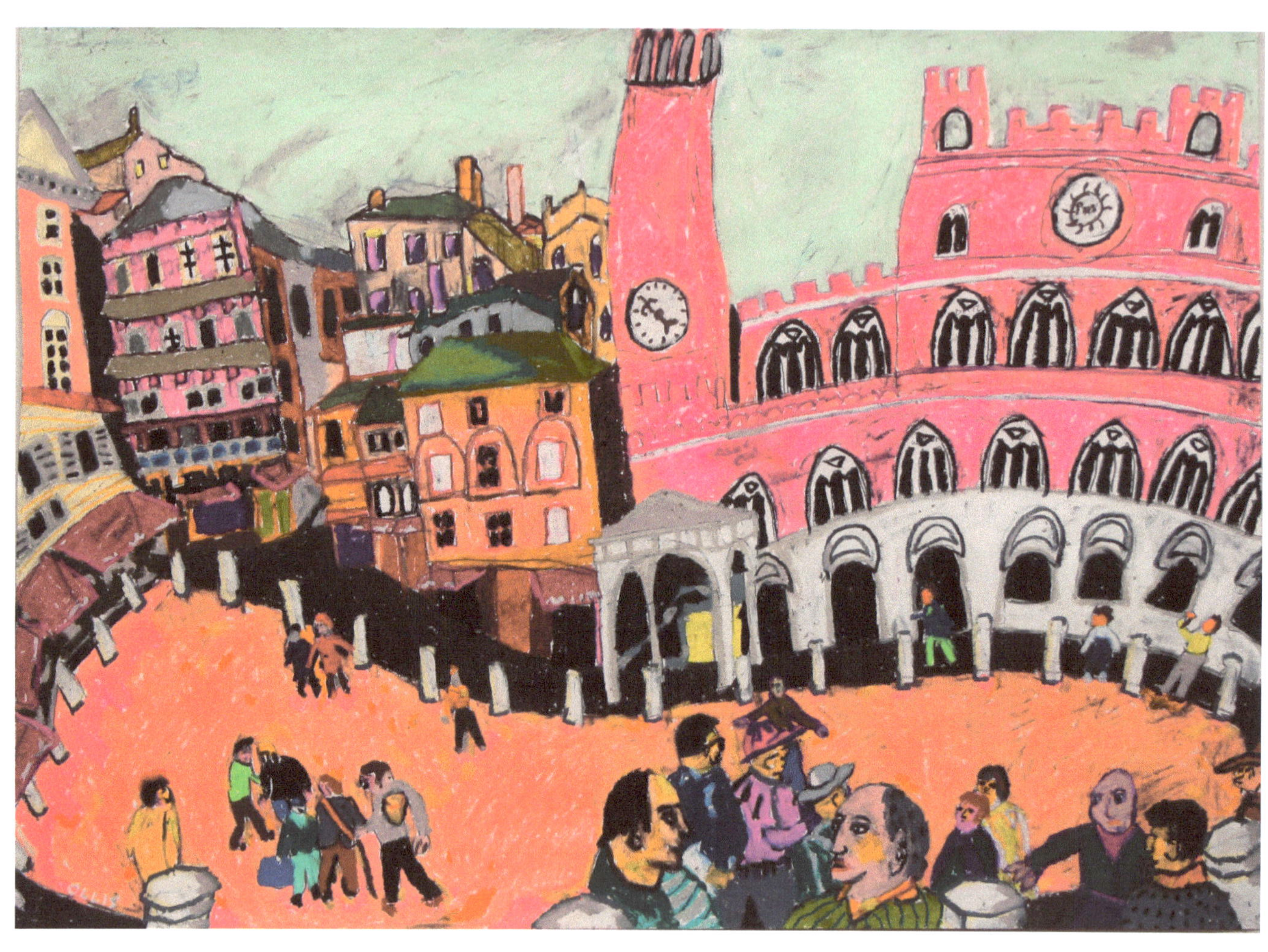

Piazza Del Campo, Siena
Oil pastel on paper
60 x 84cm
Collection of the Artist

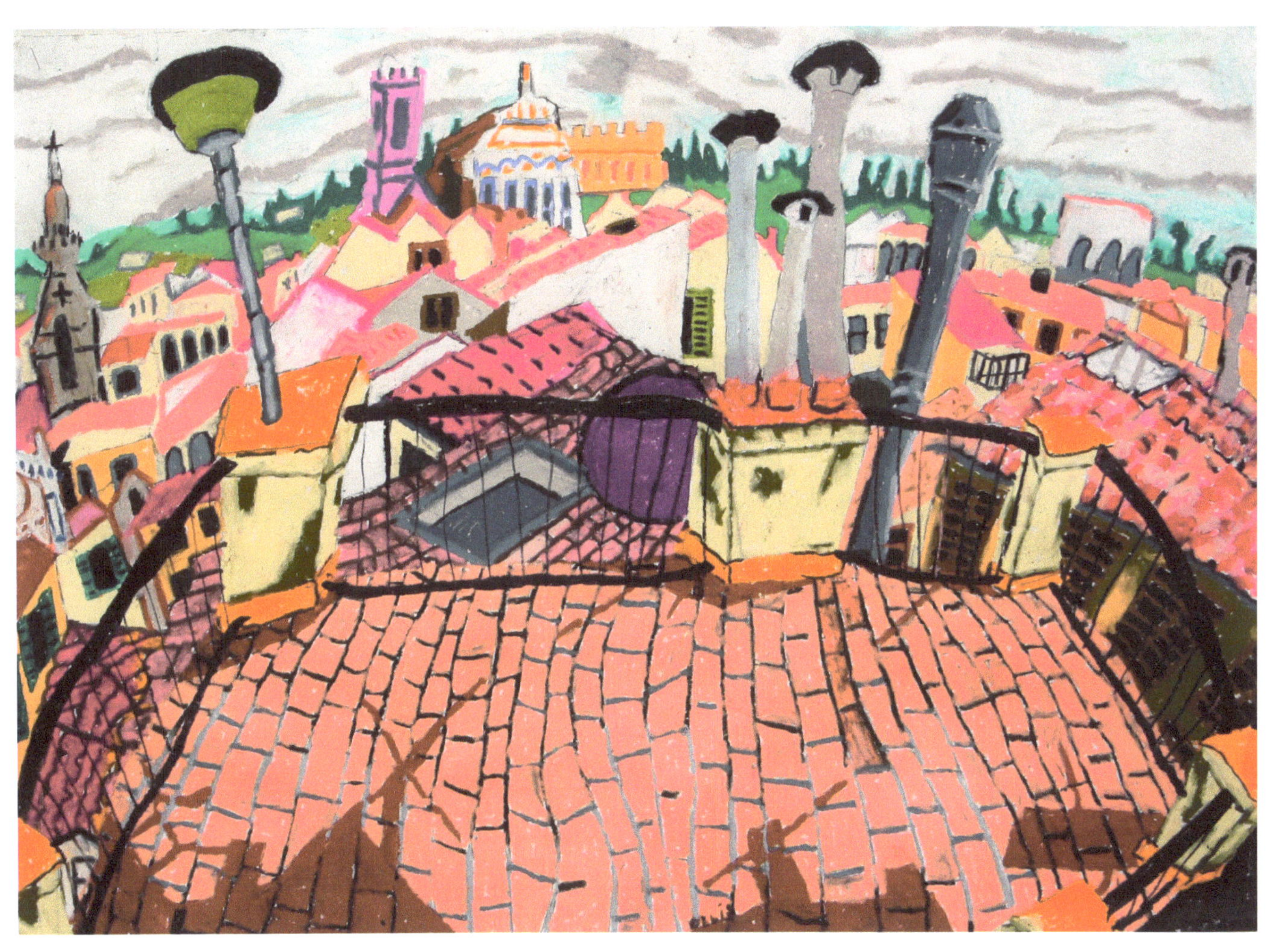

Rooftop View, Florence
Oil pastel on paper
60 x 84cm
Collection of the Artist

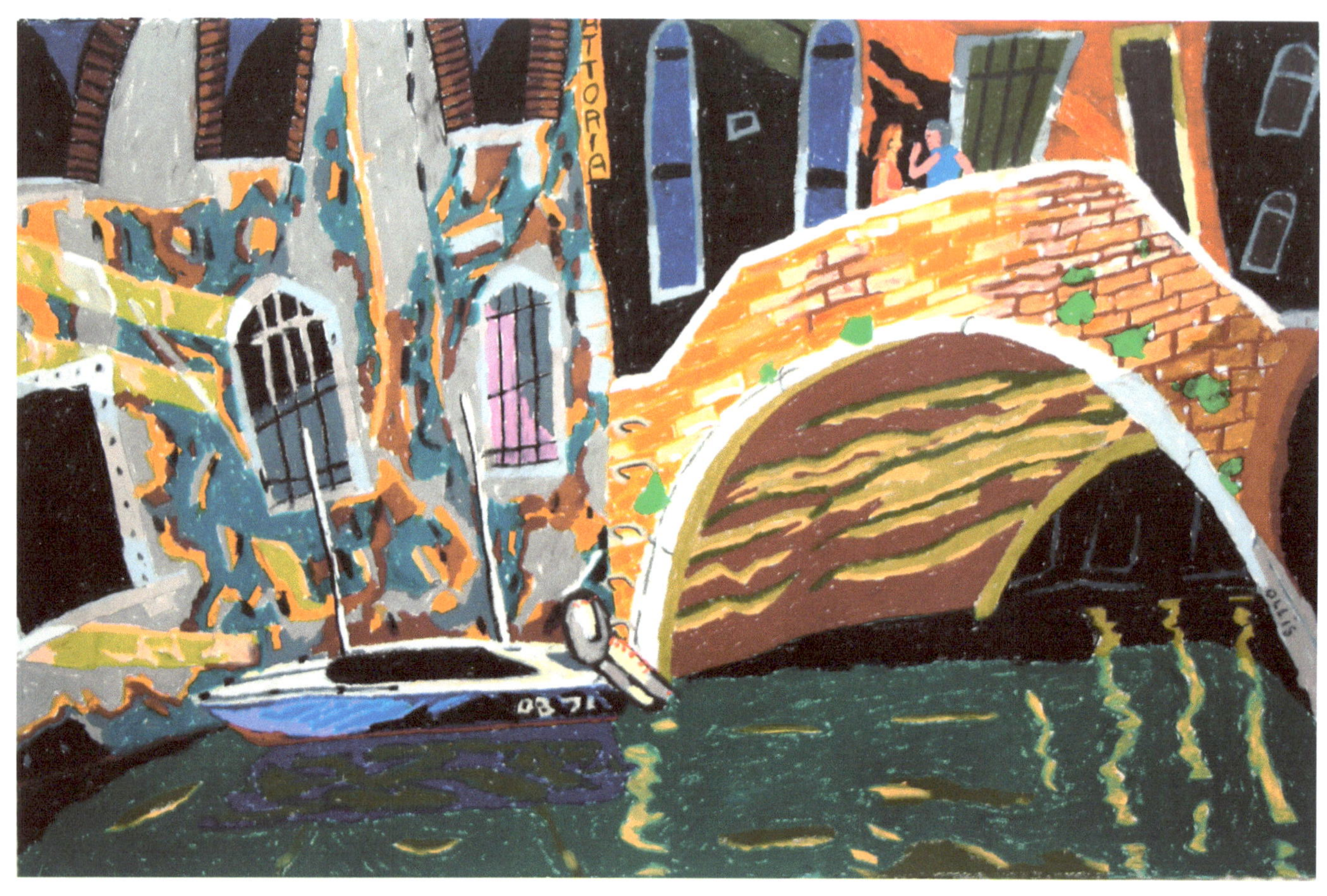

Ponte Des Gesuti, Venice
Oil pastel on paper
70 x 100cm
Collection of the Artist

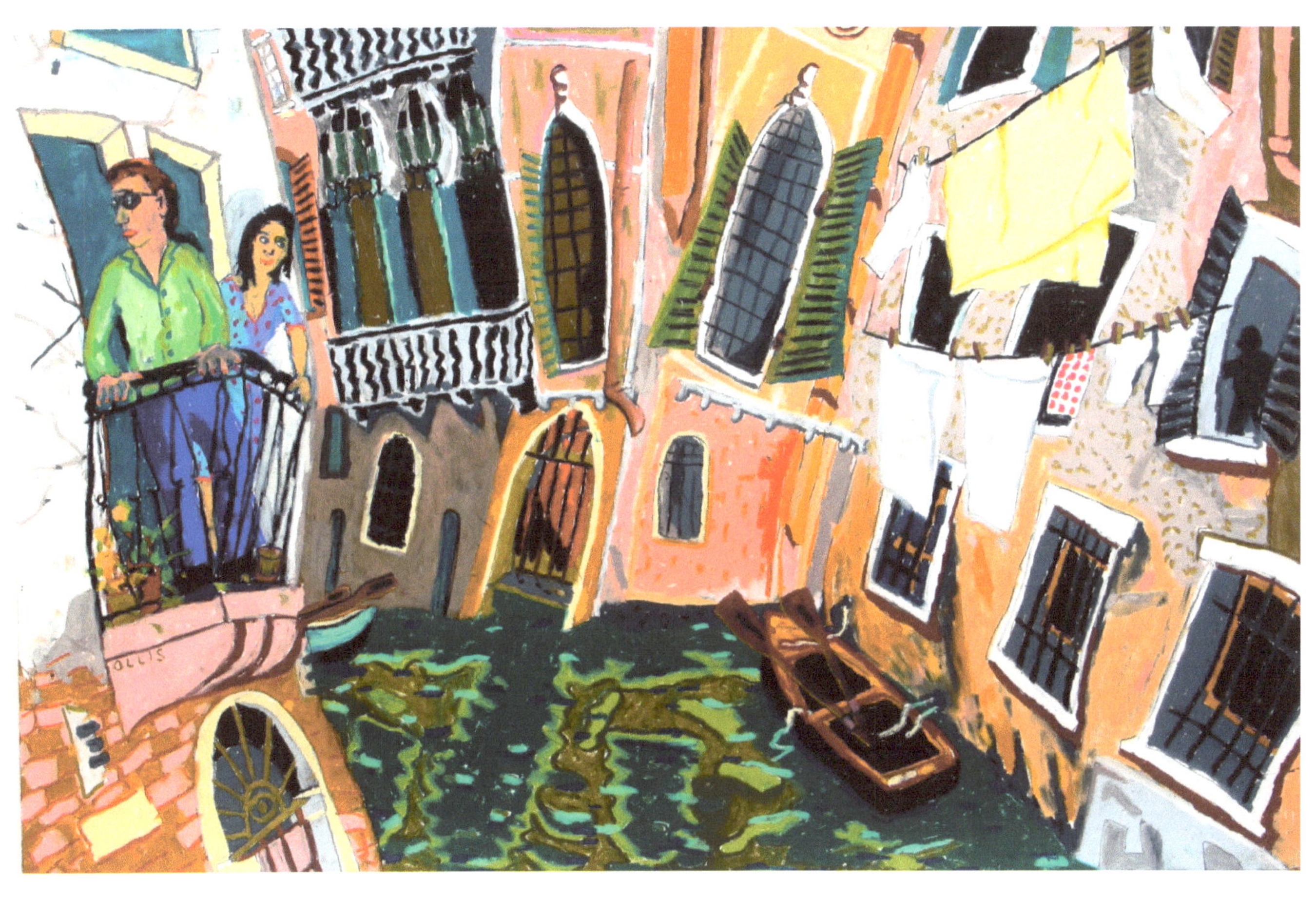

Presso Santa Maria Del Mirracoli Venice
Oil pastel on paper
70 x 100cm
Private Collection, Perth

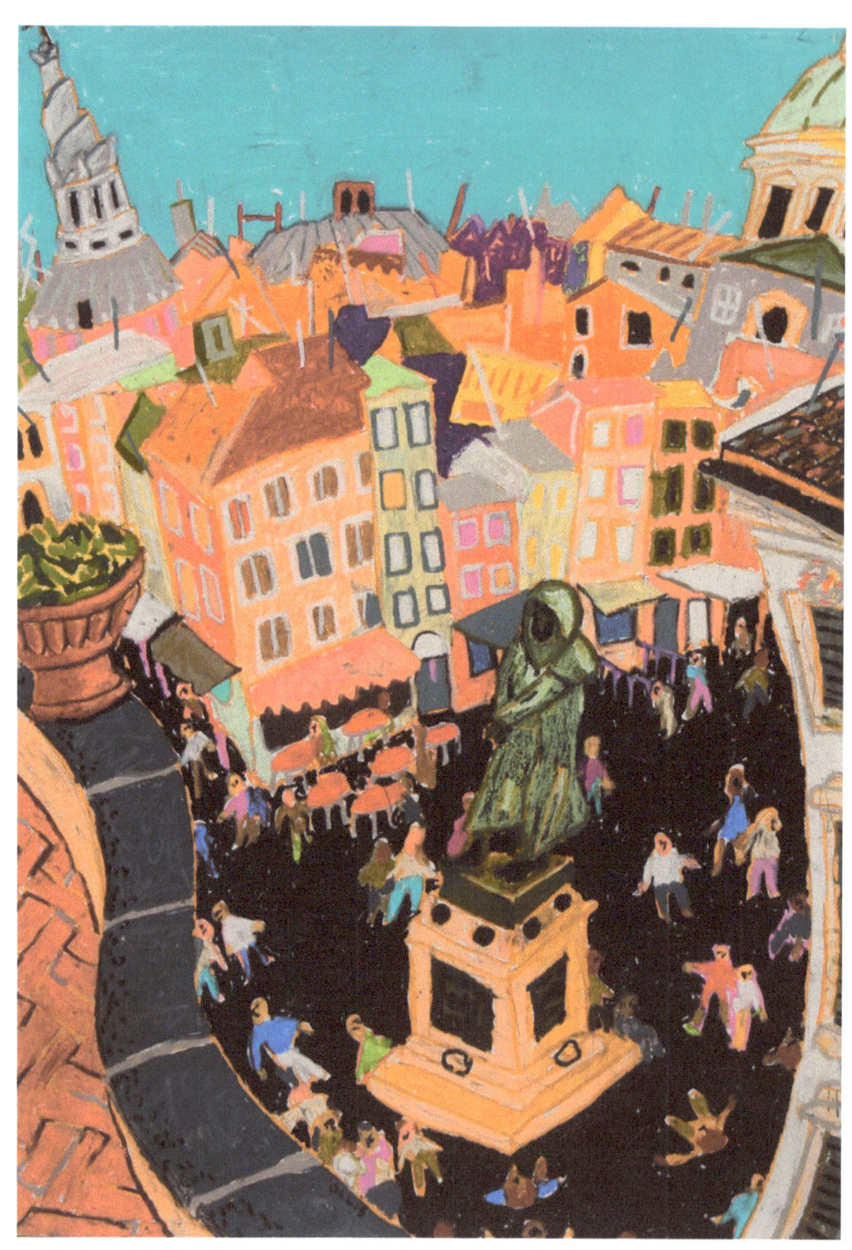

Campo De Fiori, Rome
Oil pastel on paper
84 x 60cm
Collection of the Artist

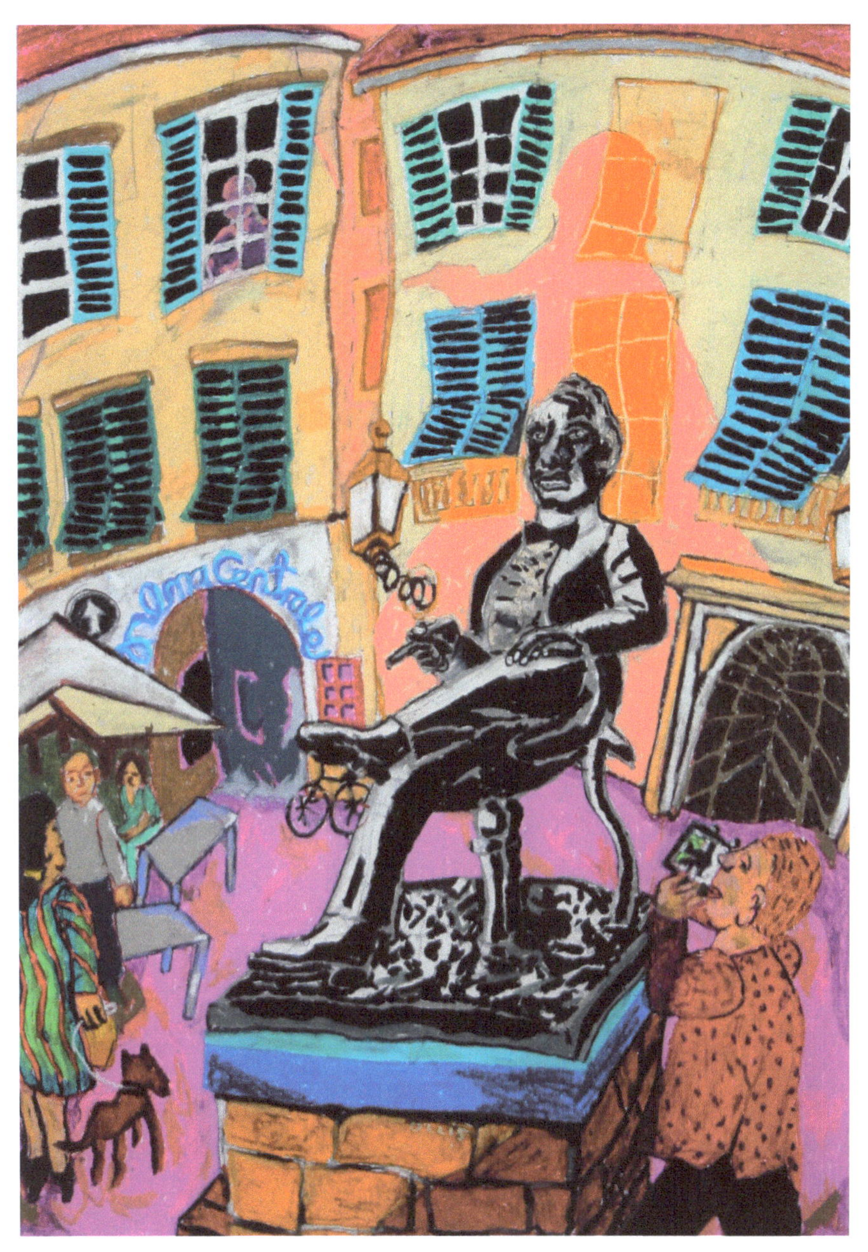

Puccini in his Square, Lucca

Oil pastel on paper

84 x 60cm

Collection of the Artist

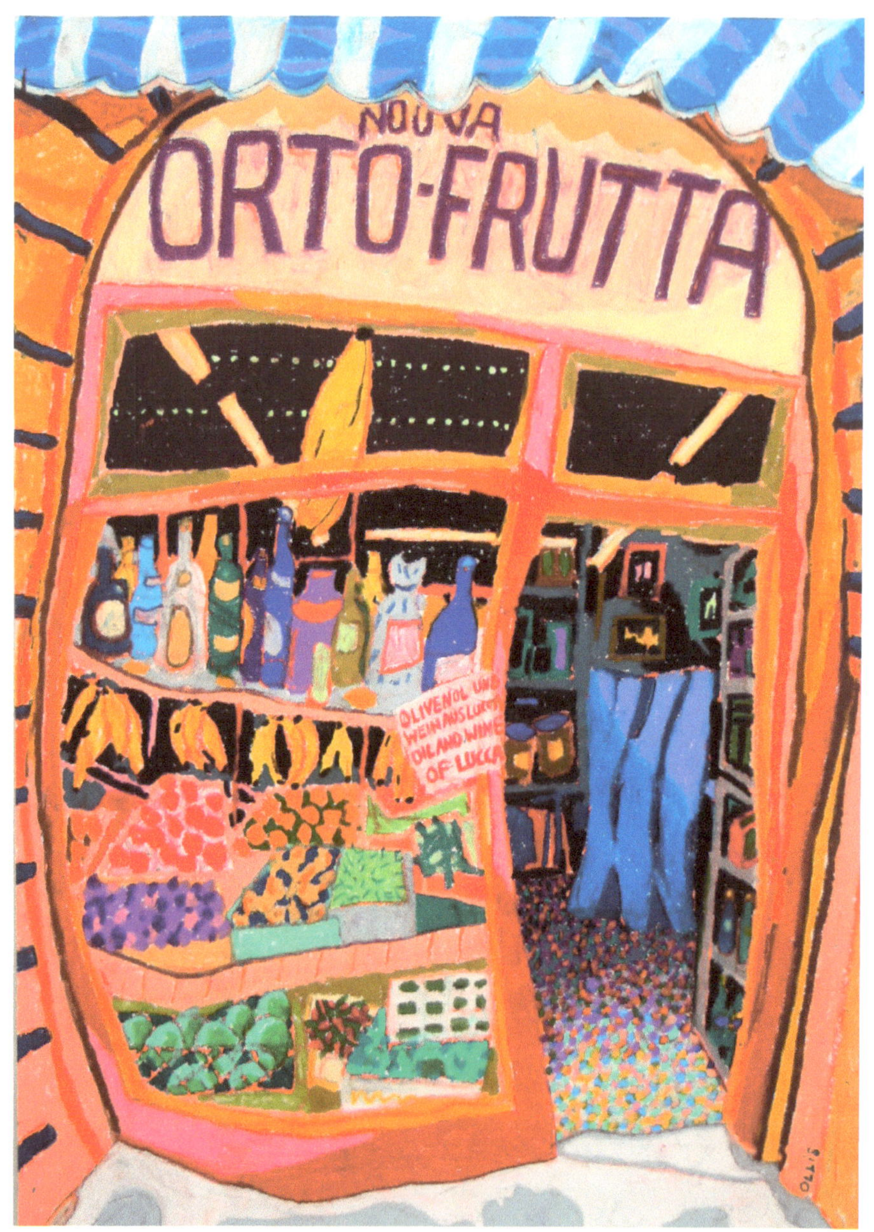

Orto Frutta
Oil pastel on paper
84 x 60cm
Collection of the Artist

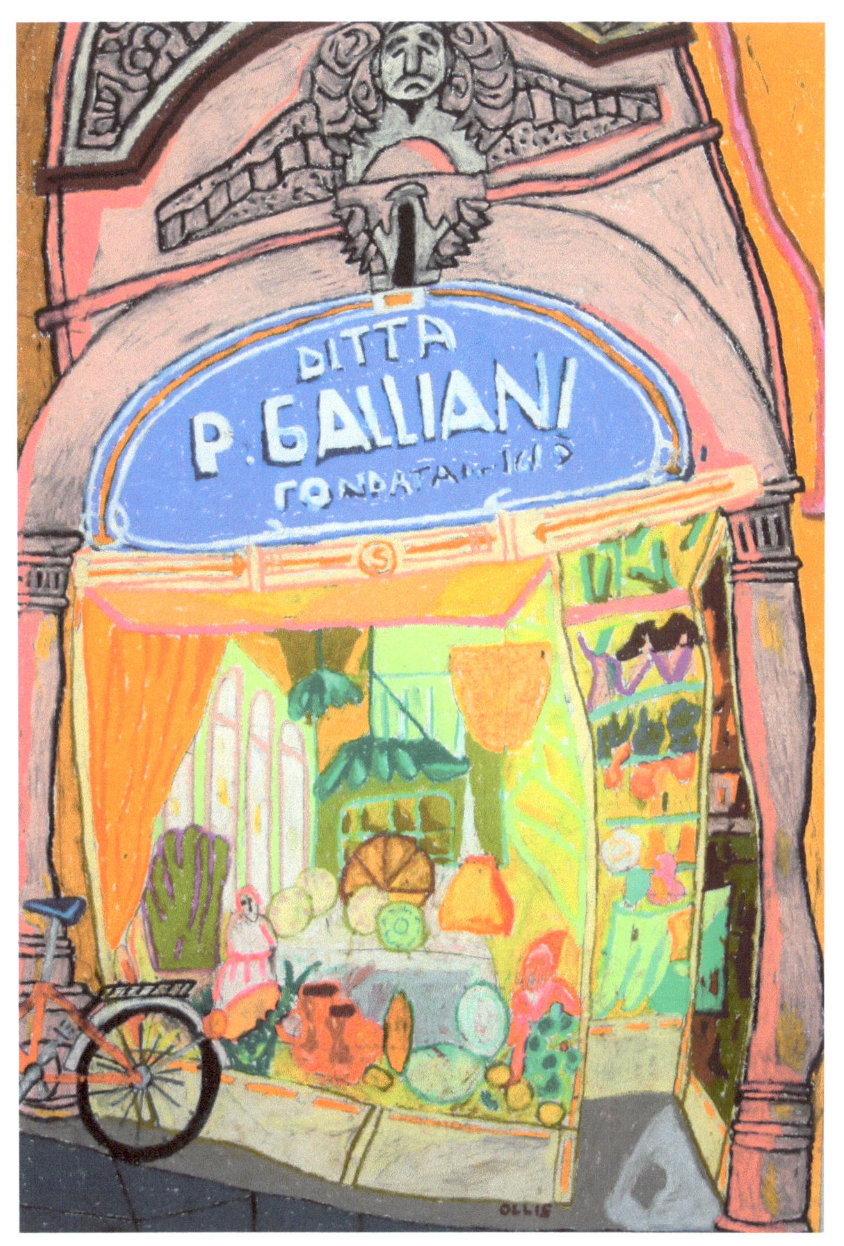

P. Galliani

Pastel on paper

84 x 60cm

Collection of the Artist

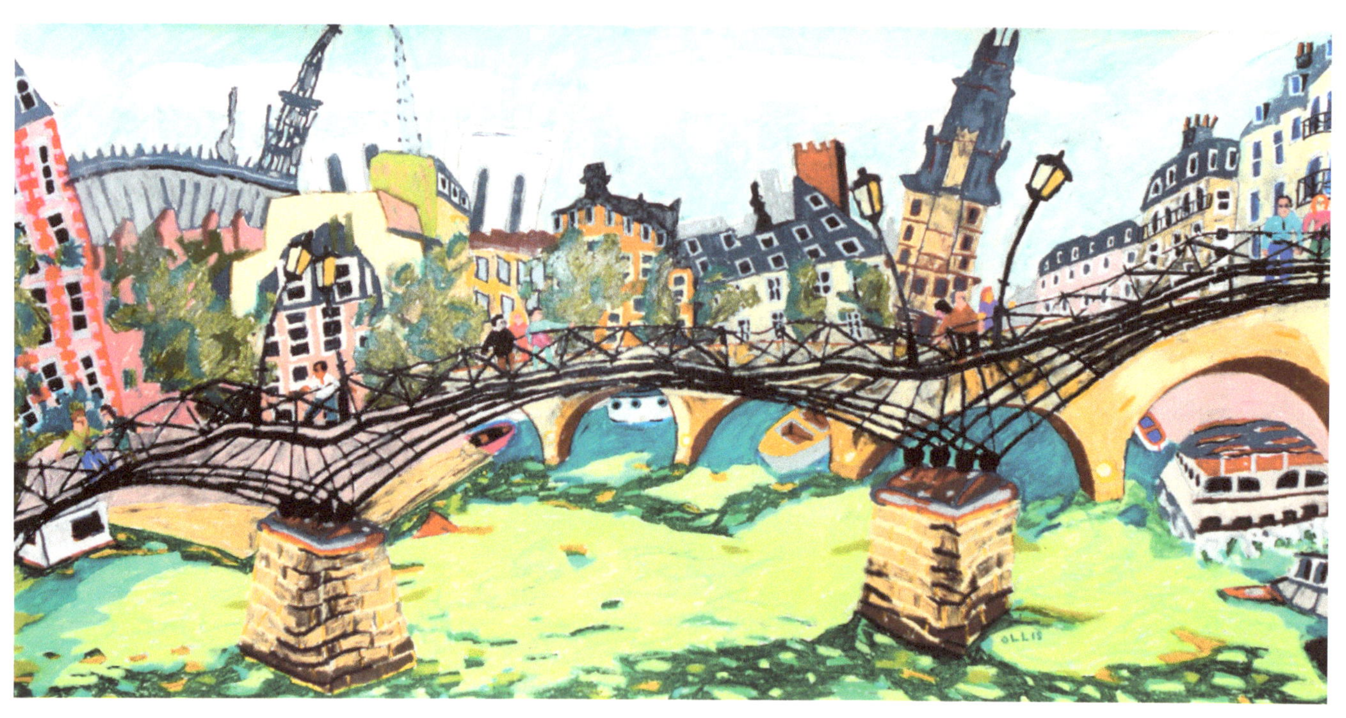

The Pont Des Arts, Paris 2011
Oil pastel on paper
76 x 150cm
Collection of the Artist

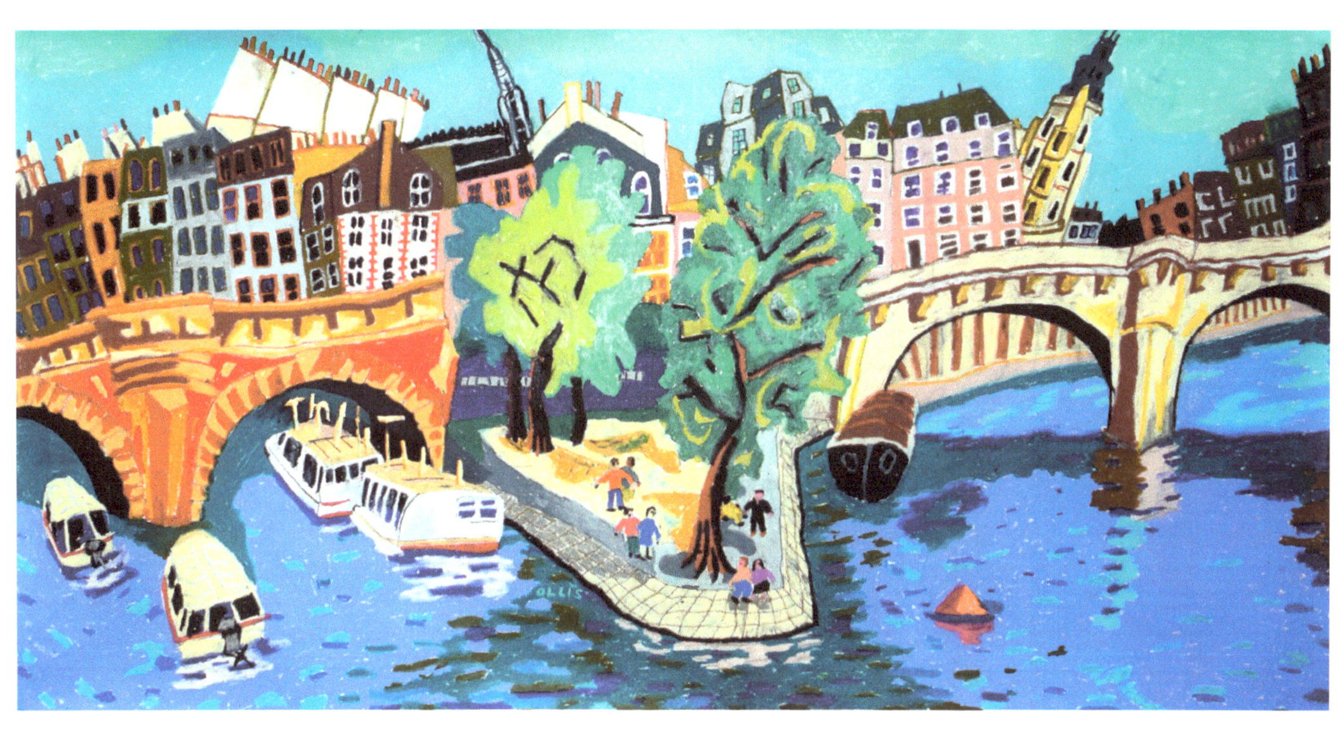

L'ile De La Cite, Paris 2011
Oil pastel on paper
76 x 150cm
Collection of the Artist

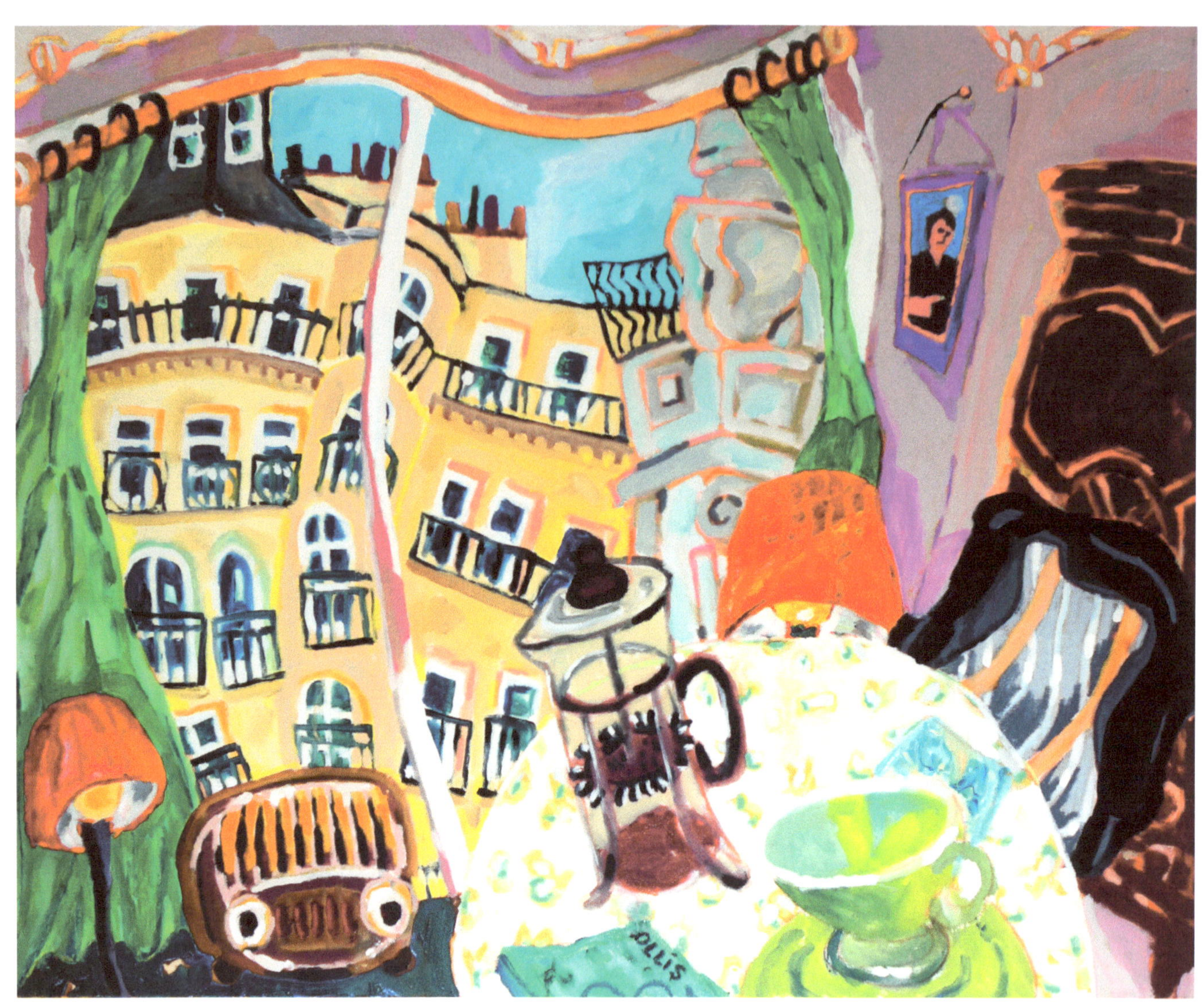

Paris View with Lampshades and Radio
Oil on canvas
100 x 125cm
Collection of the Artist

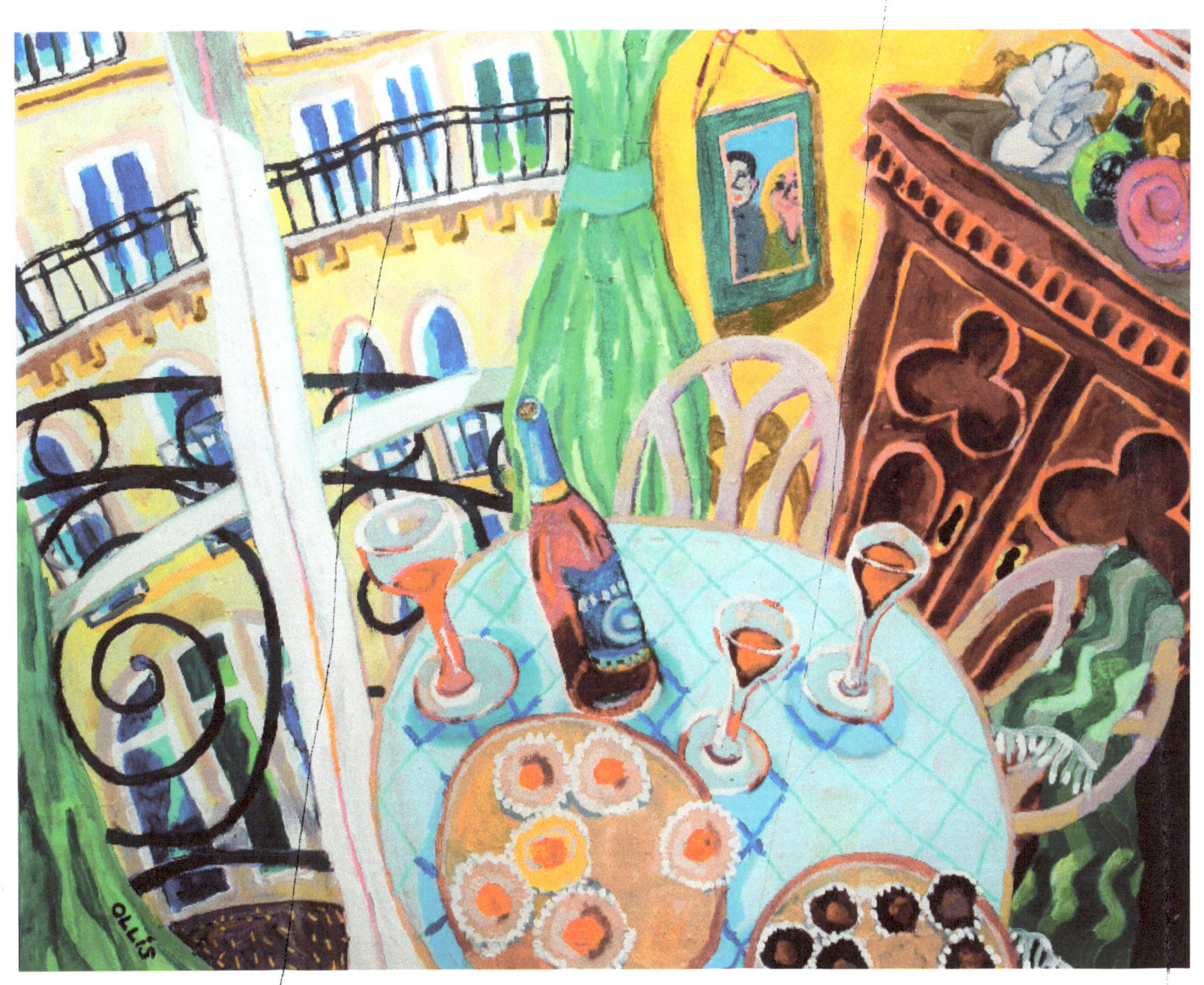

Paris View with Blue Tablecloths and Cakes
Oil on canvas
100 x 125cm
Collection of the Artist

Major Works 1980 - 2011

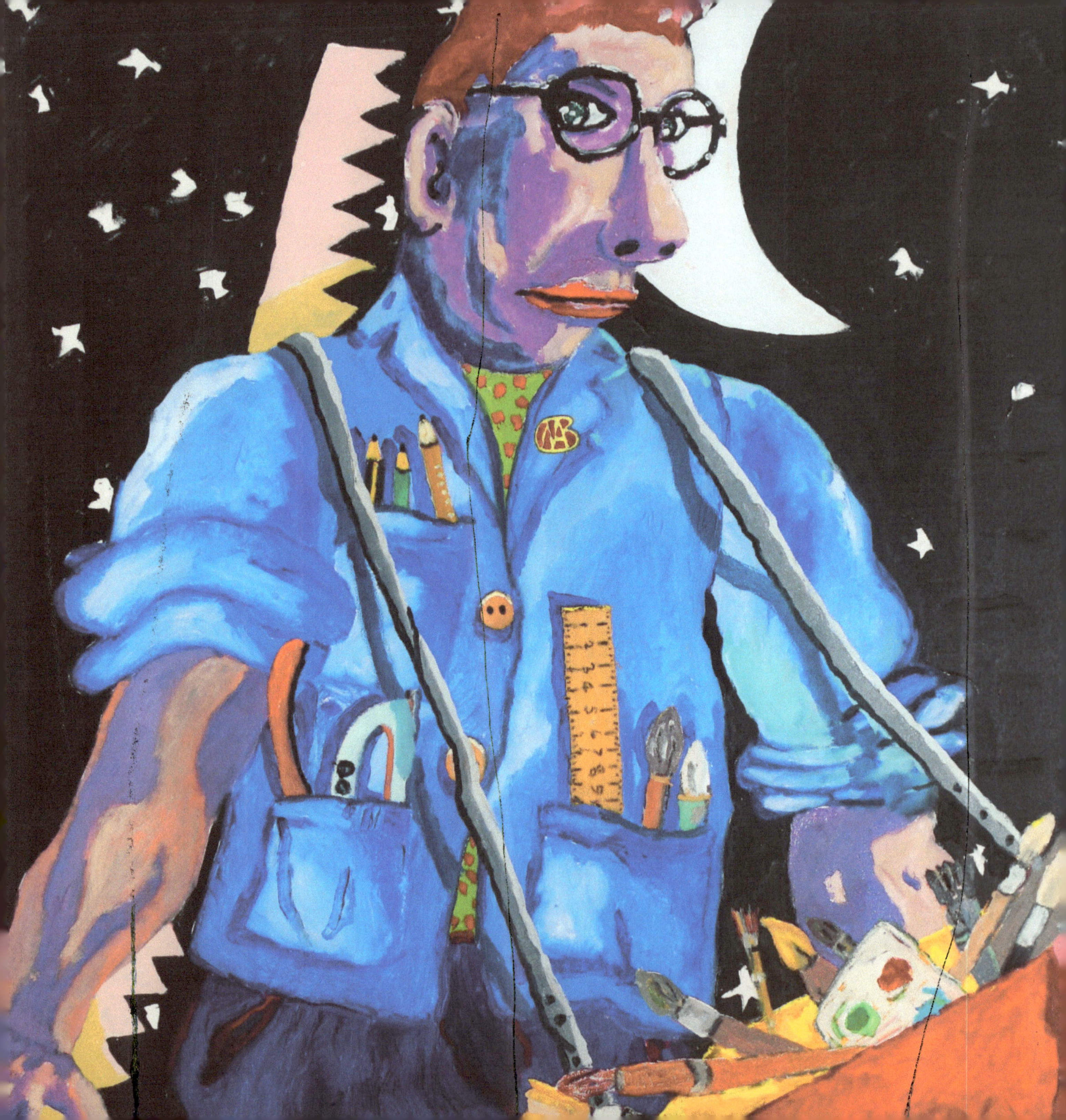

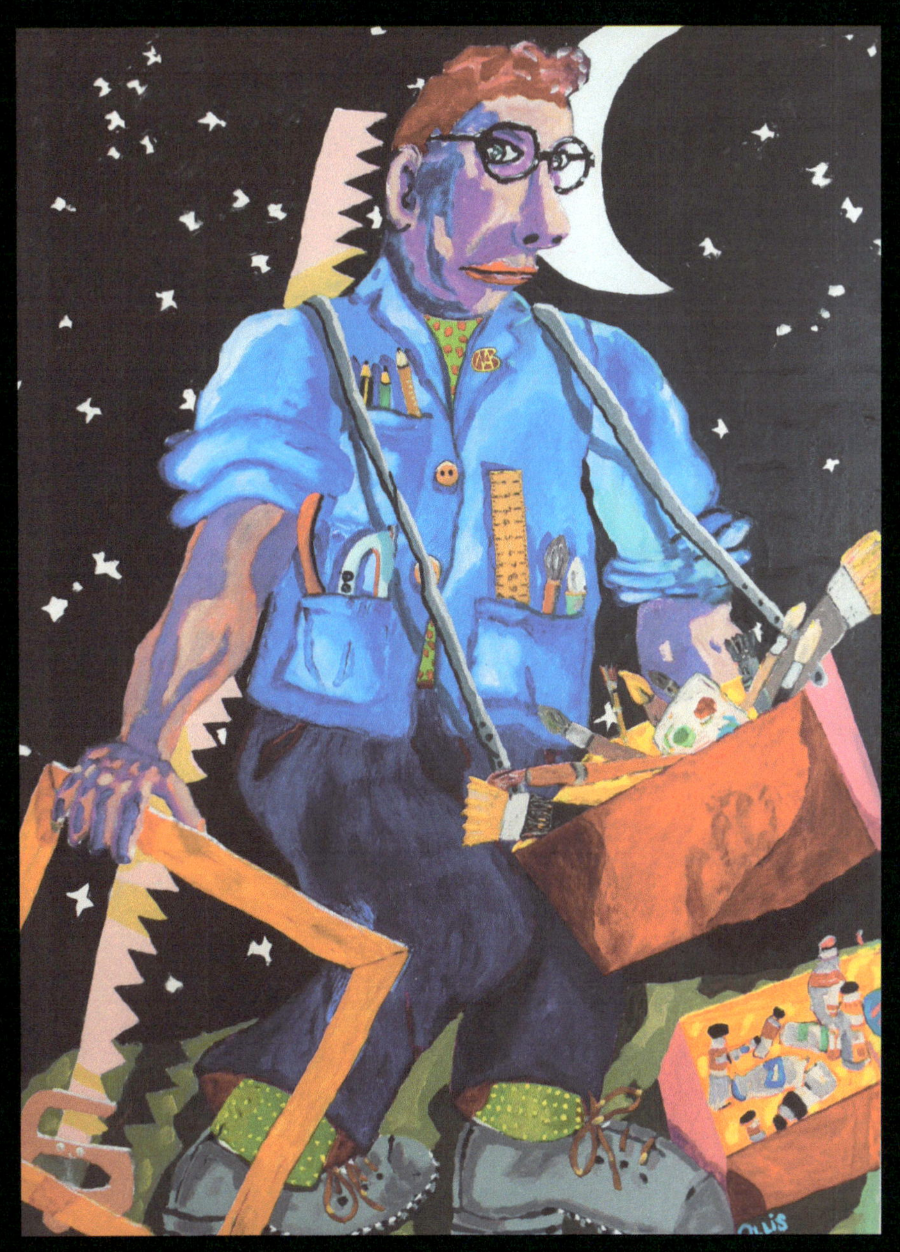

Self Portrait at the Crossroads
Oil on canvas
168 x 122cm
Collection of the Artist

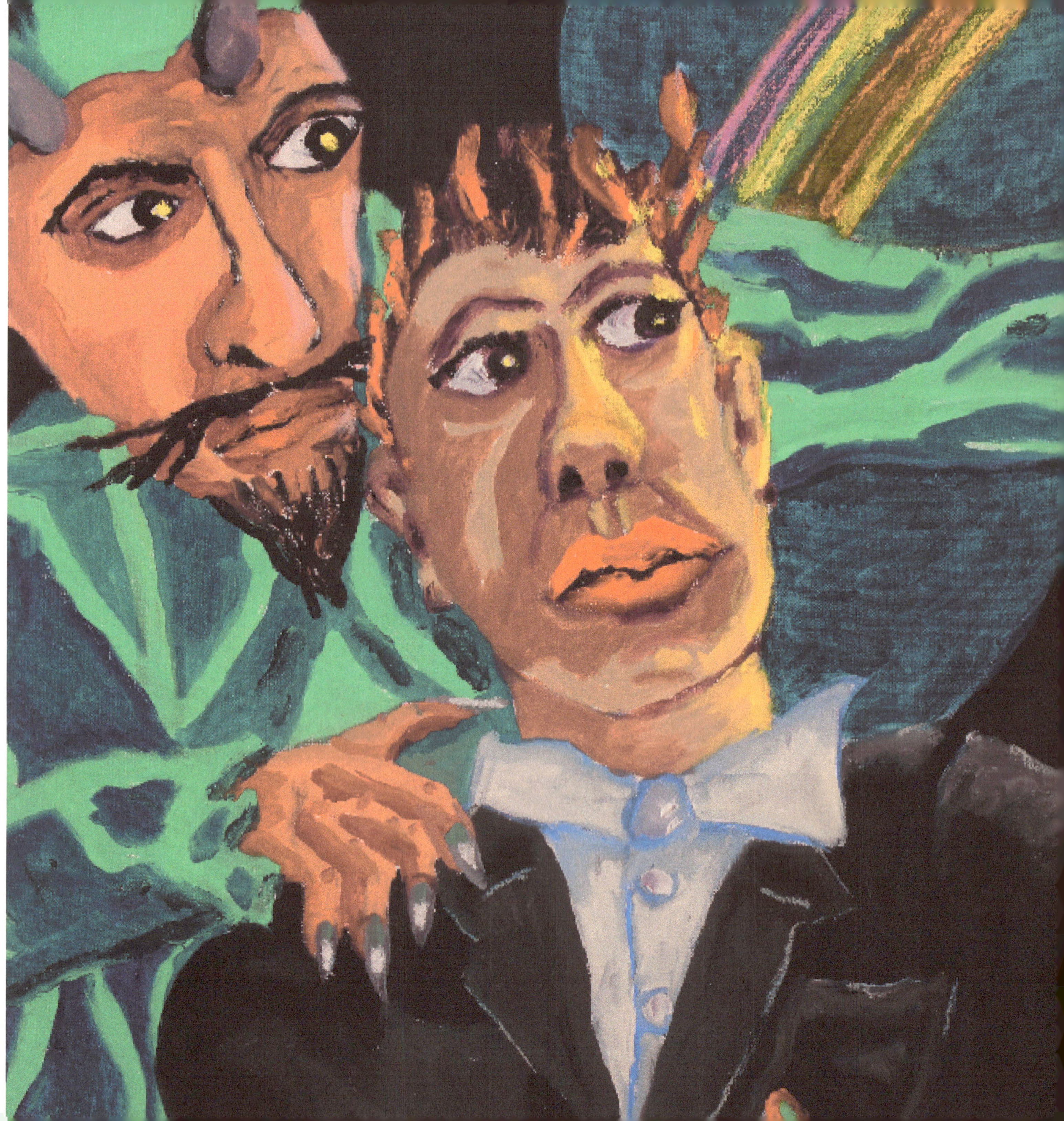

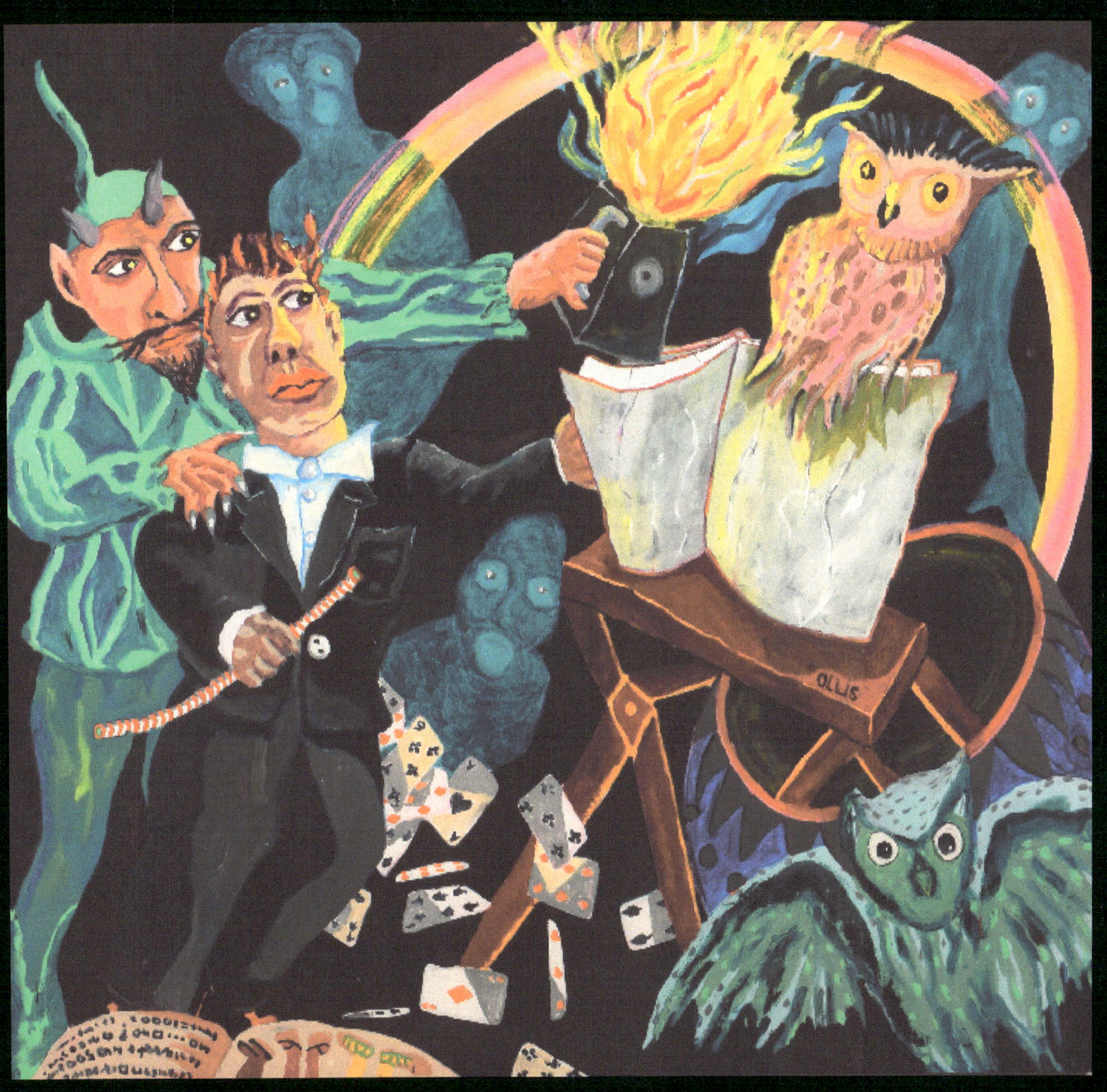

Black Magic
Oil on canvas
186 x 174cm
Collection of the Artist

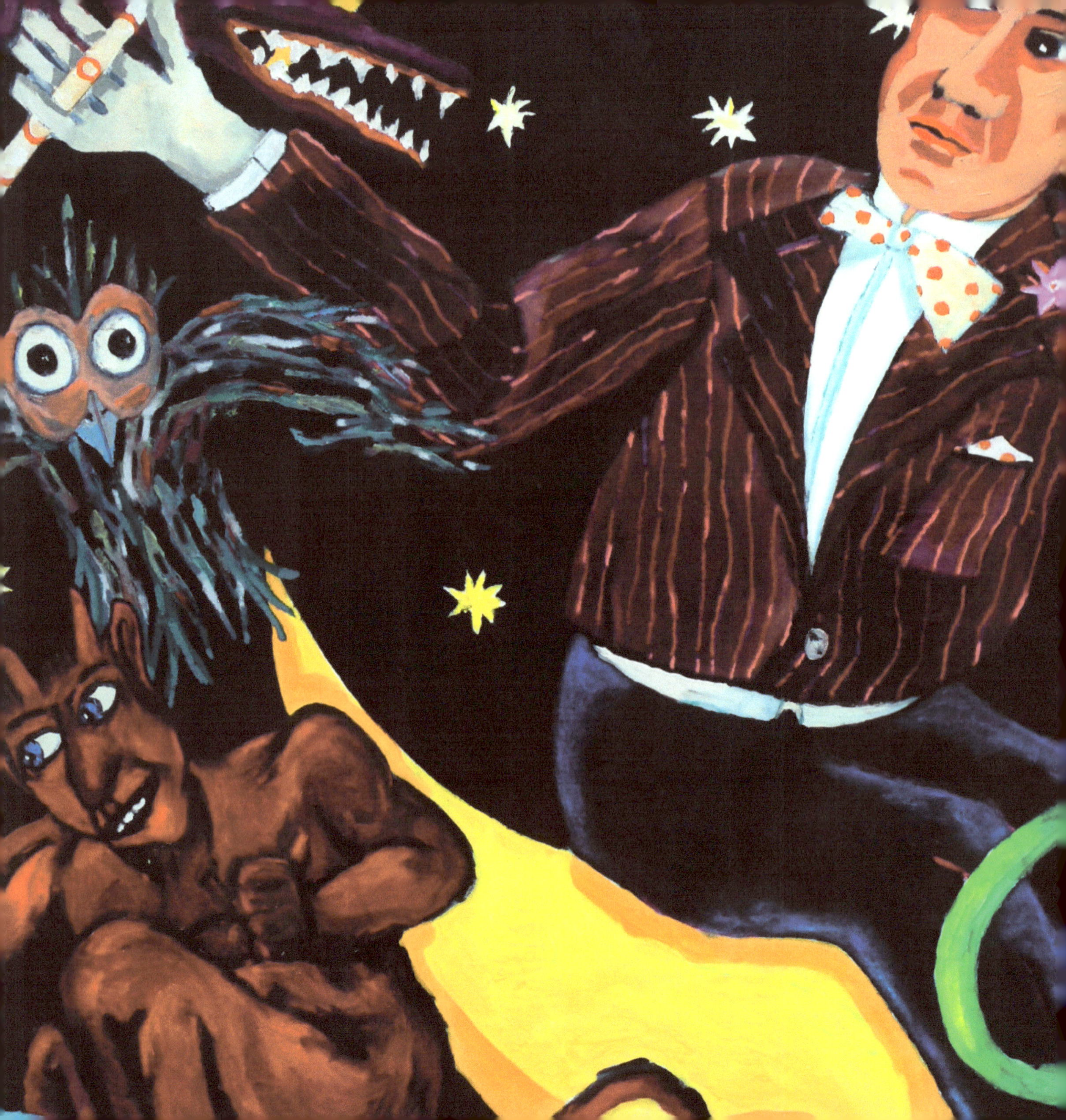

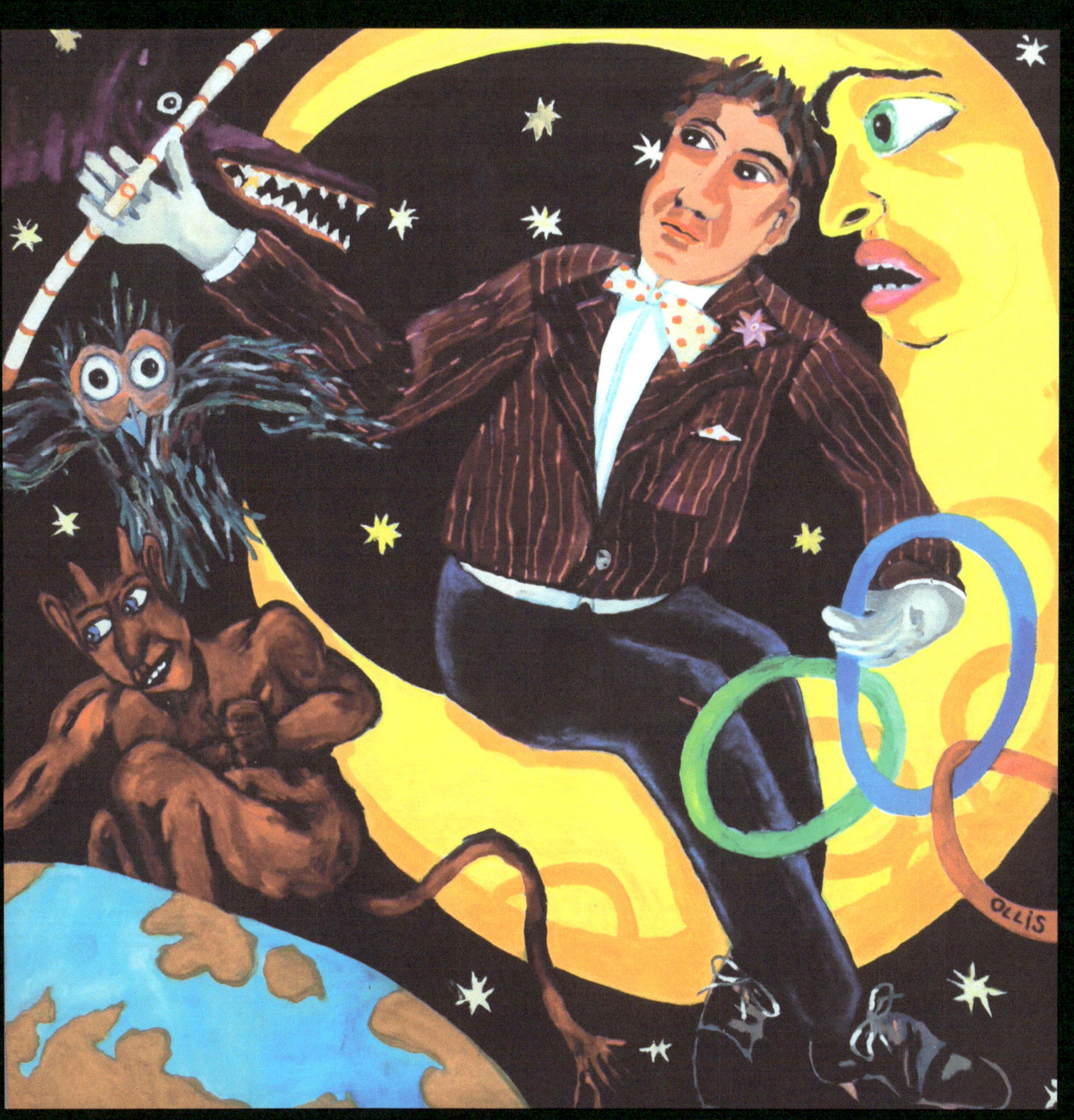

Moon and Magician
Oil on canvas
175 x 176cm
Collection of the Artist

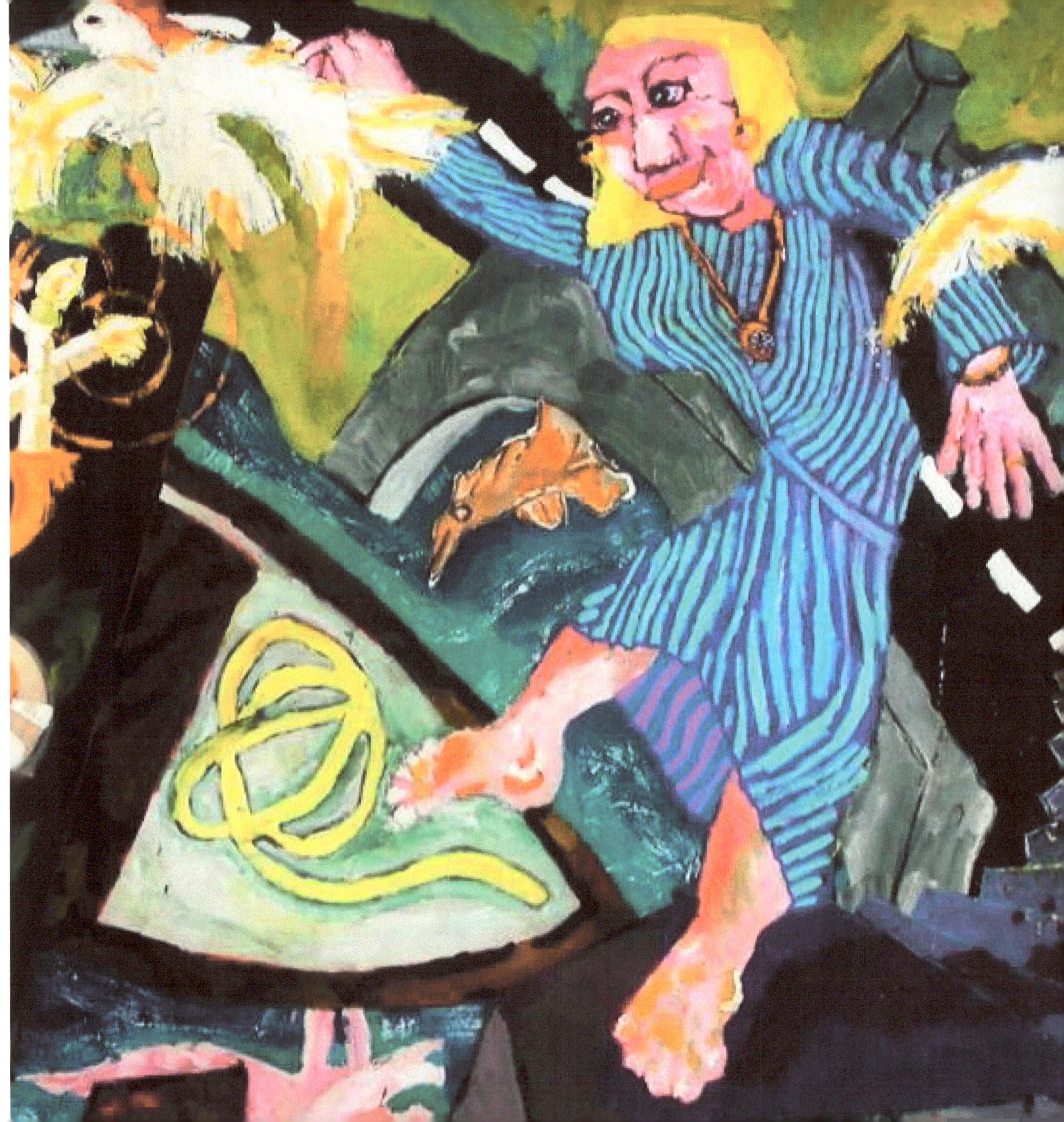

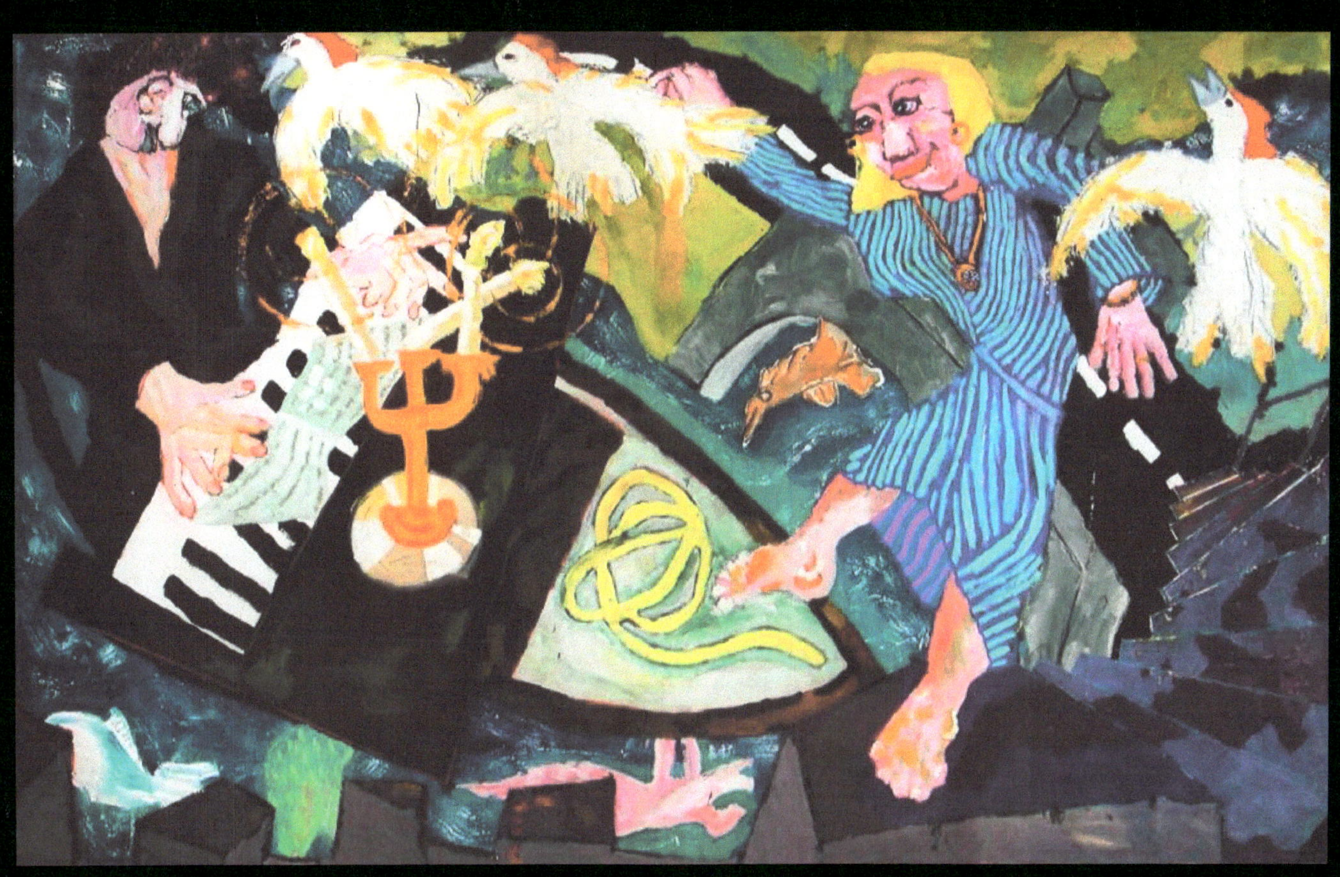

Enchantment

Oil on canvas

180 x 320cm

Collection of the Artist

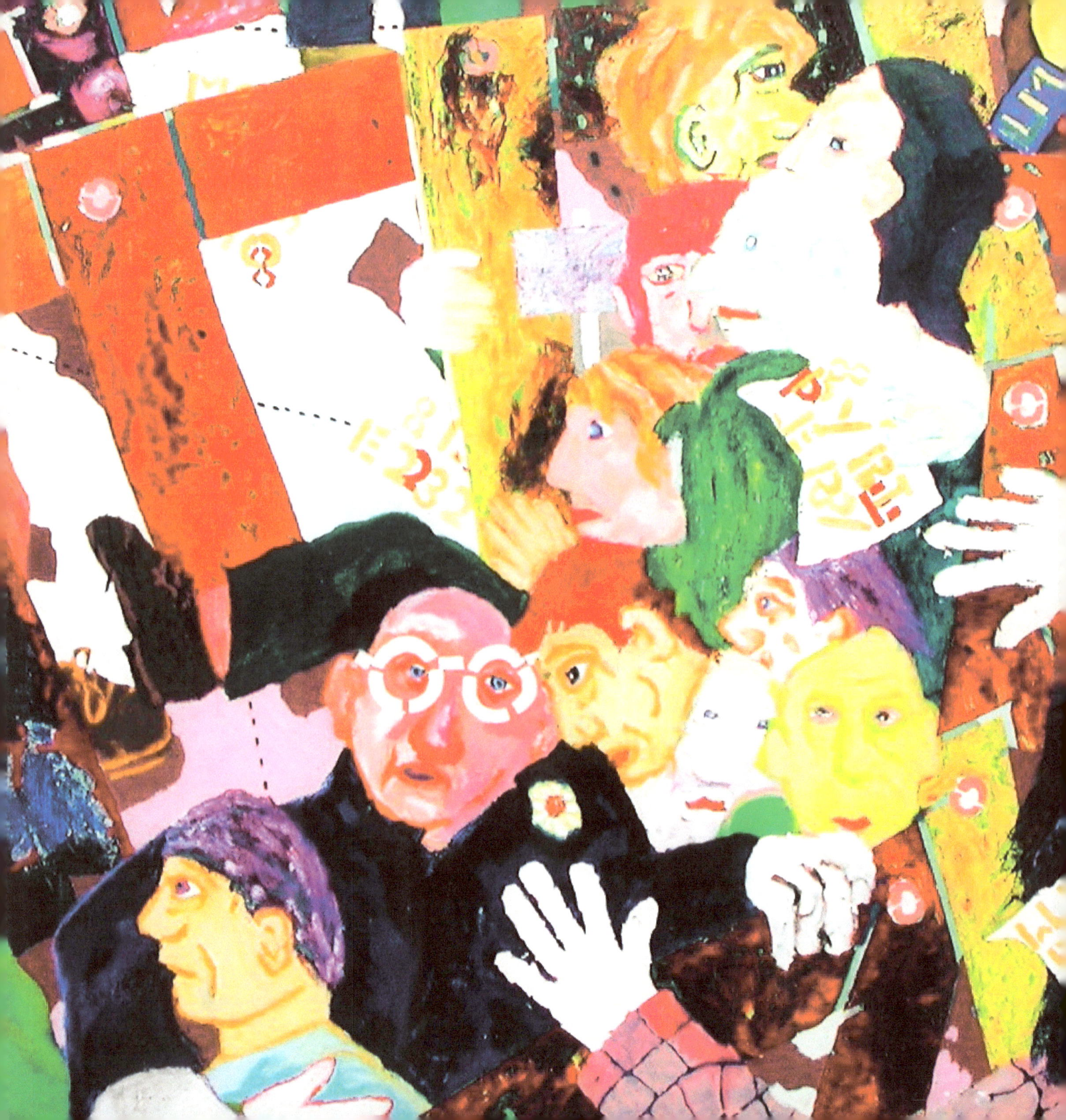

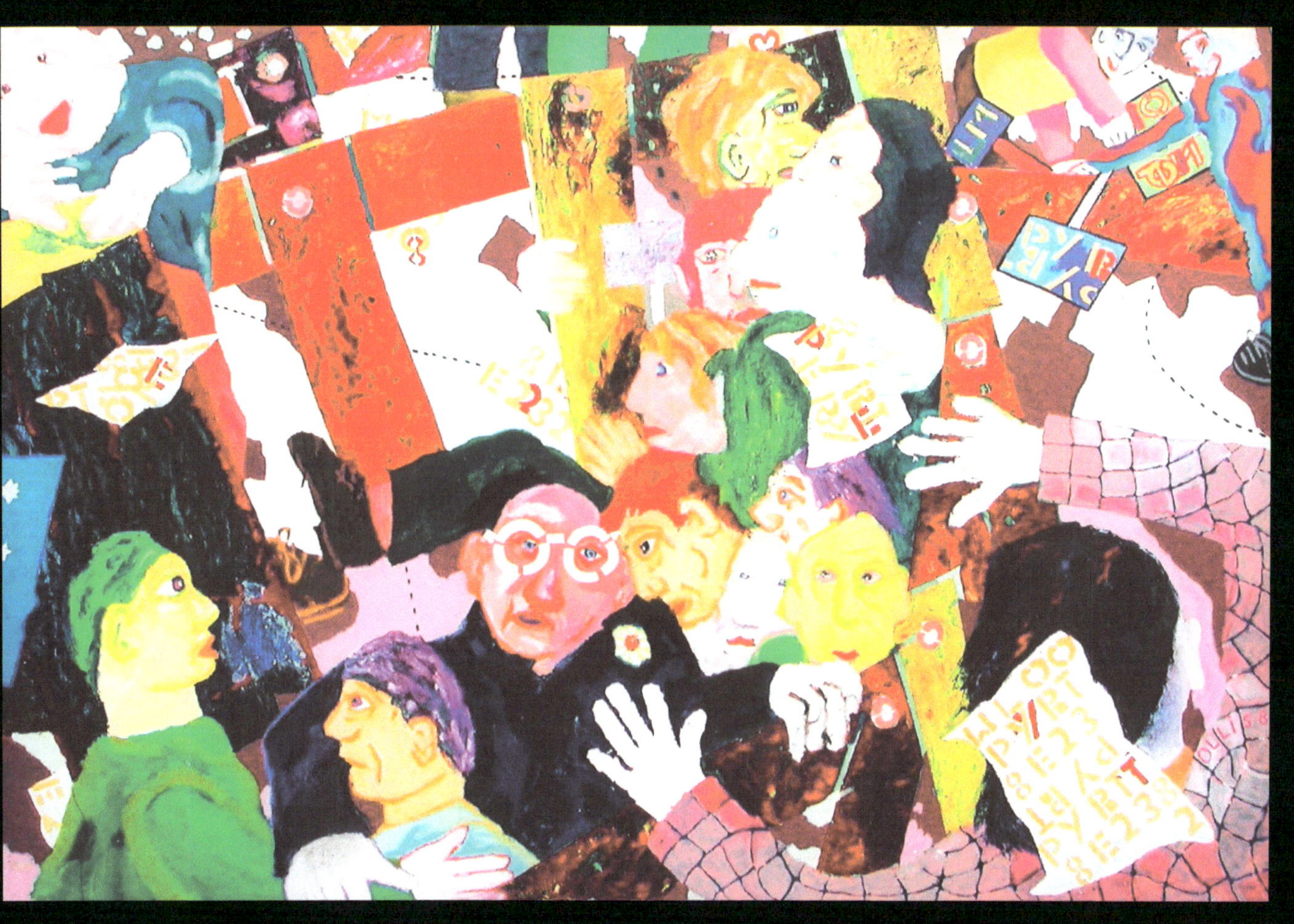

Speaker's Corner

Oil on canvas

190 x 300cm

Collection of the Artist

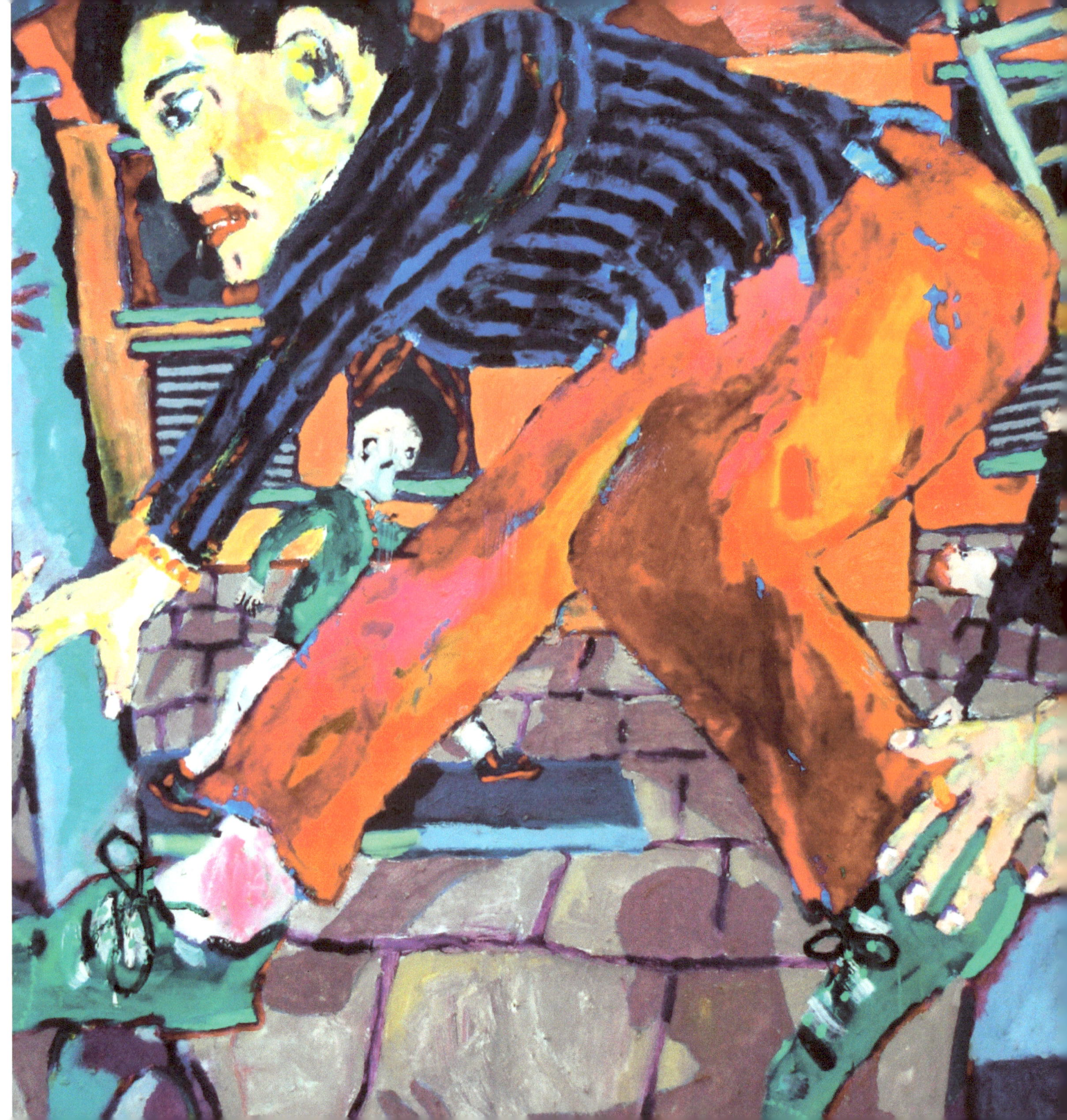

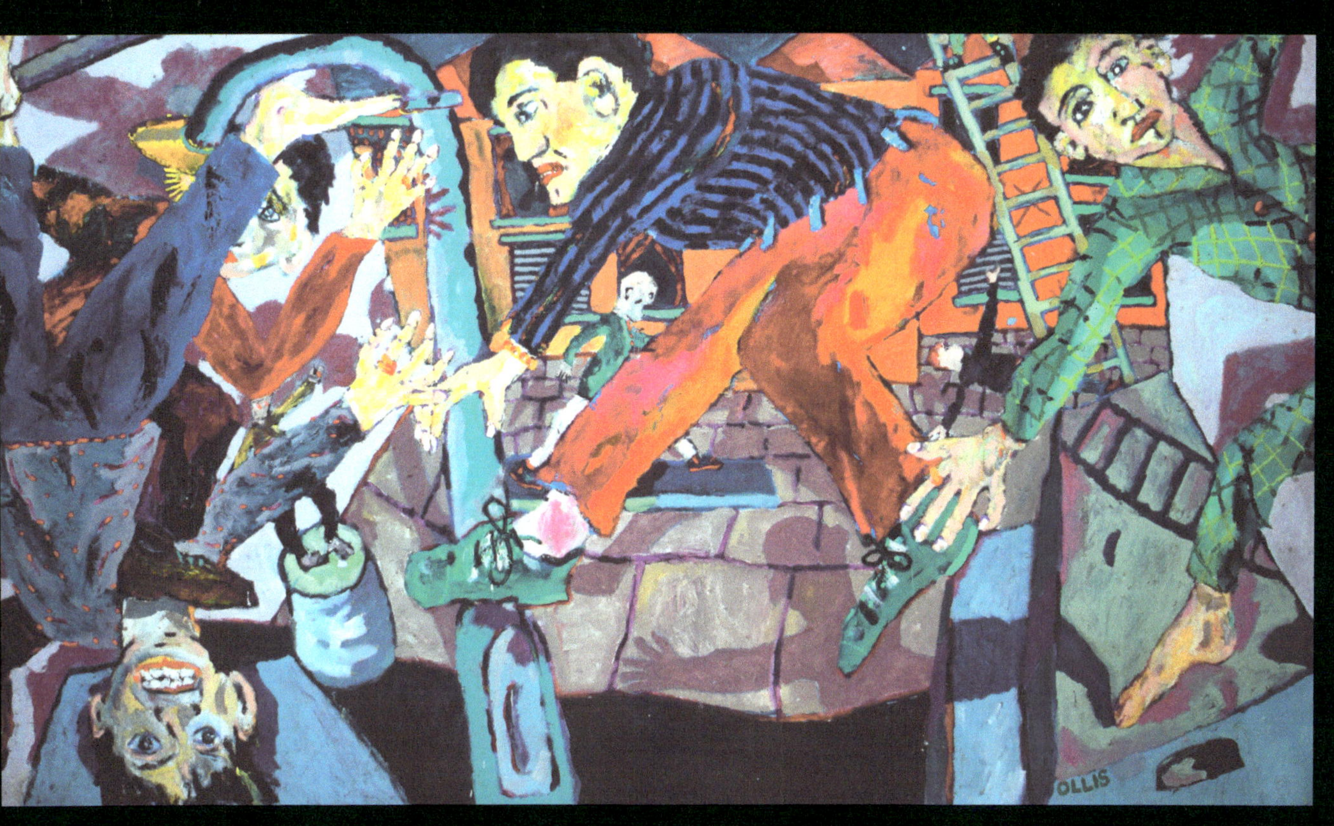

Cha Cha Cha

Oil on canvas

180 x 310cm

Collection of the Artist

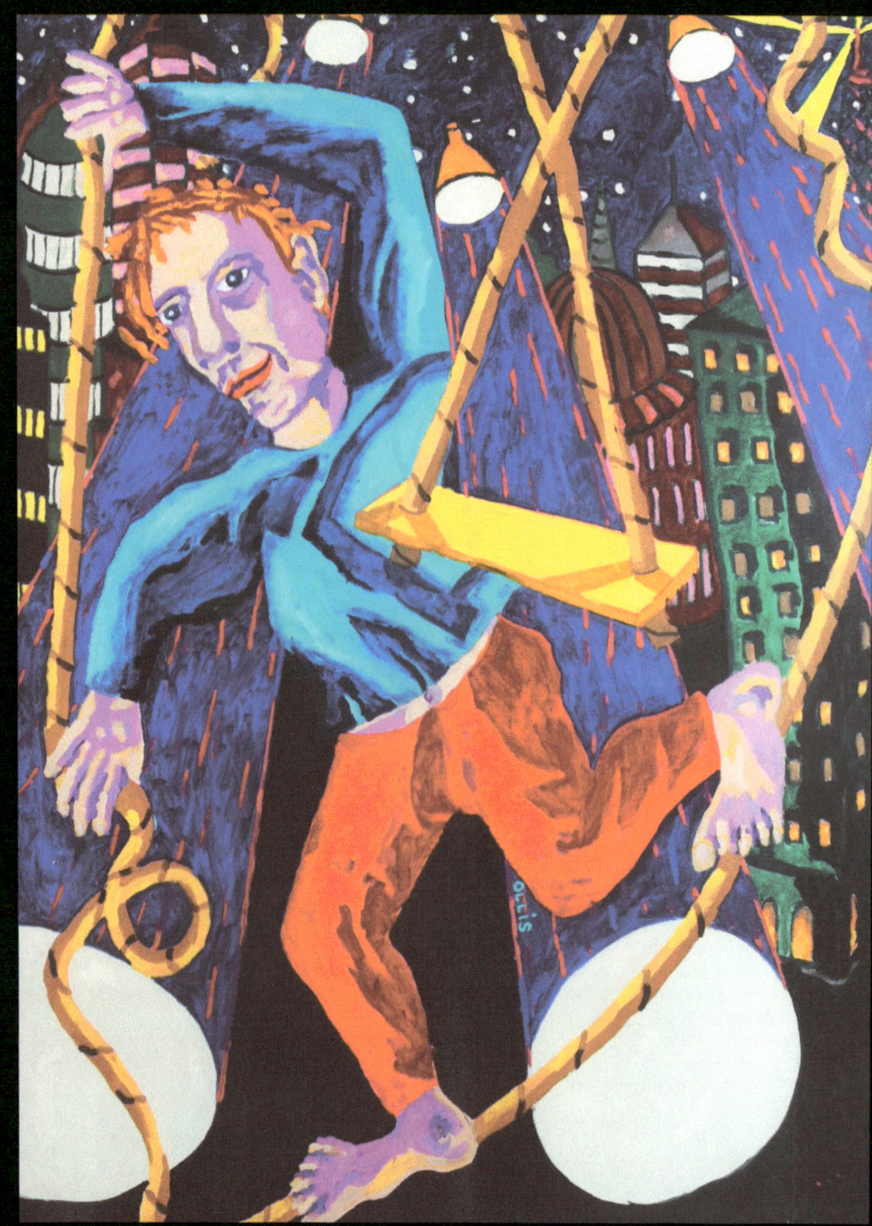

Traversing the City

Oil on canvas

122 x 168cm
Collection of the Artist

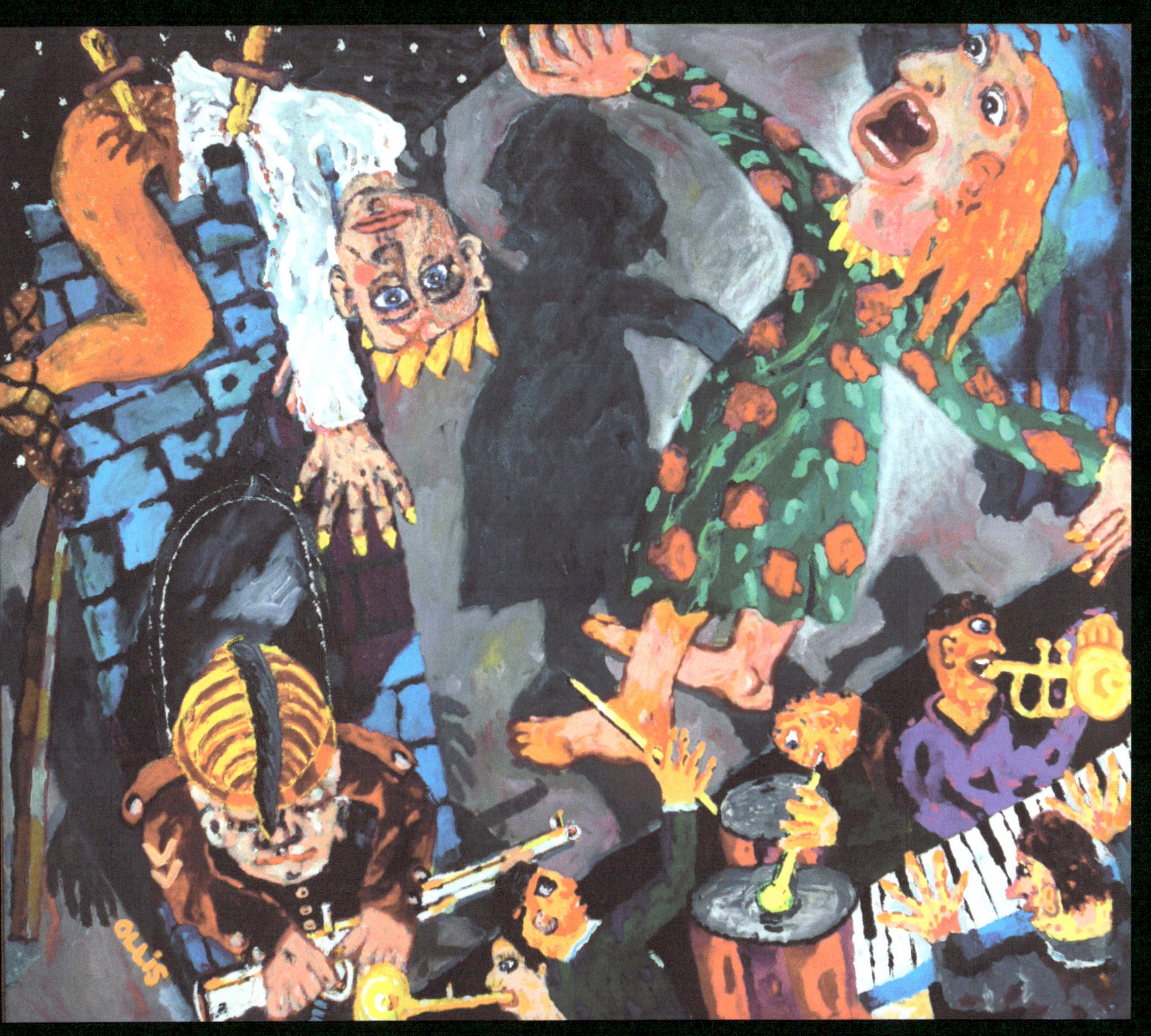

Diva
Oil on canvas
206 x 177cm
Collection of the Artist

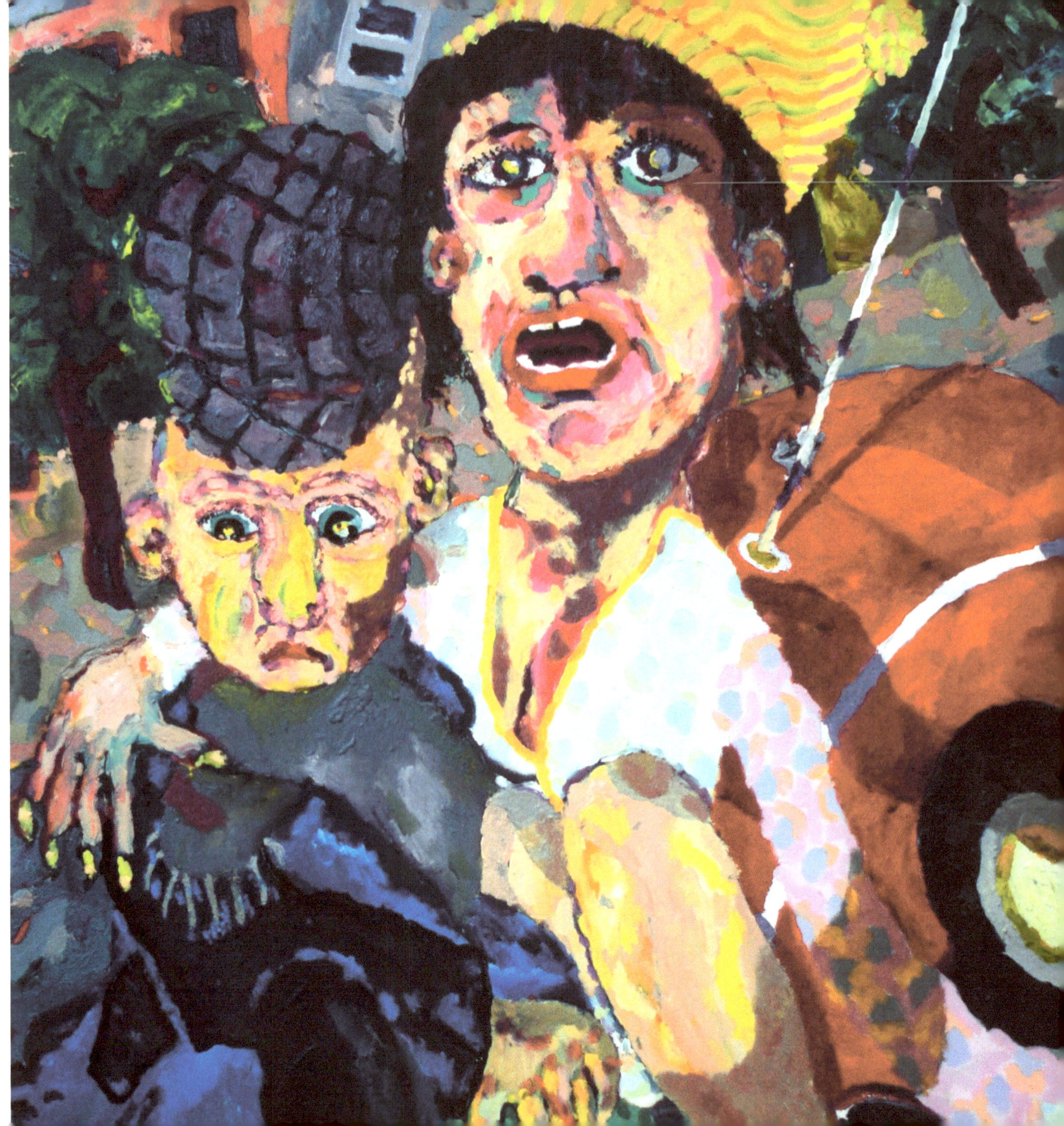

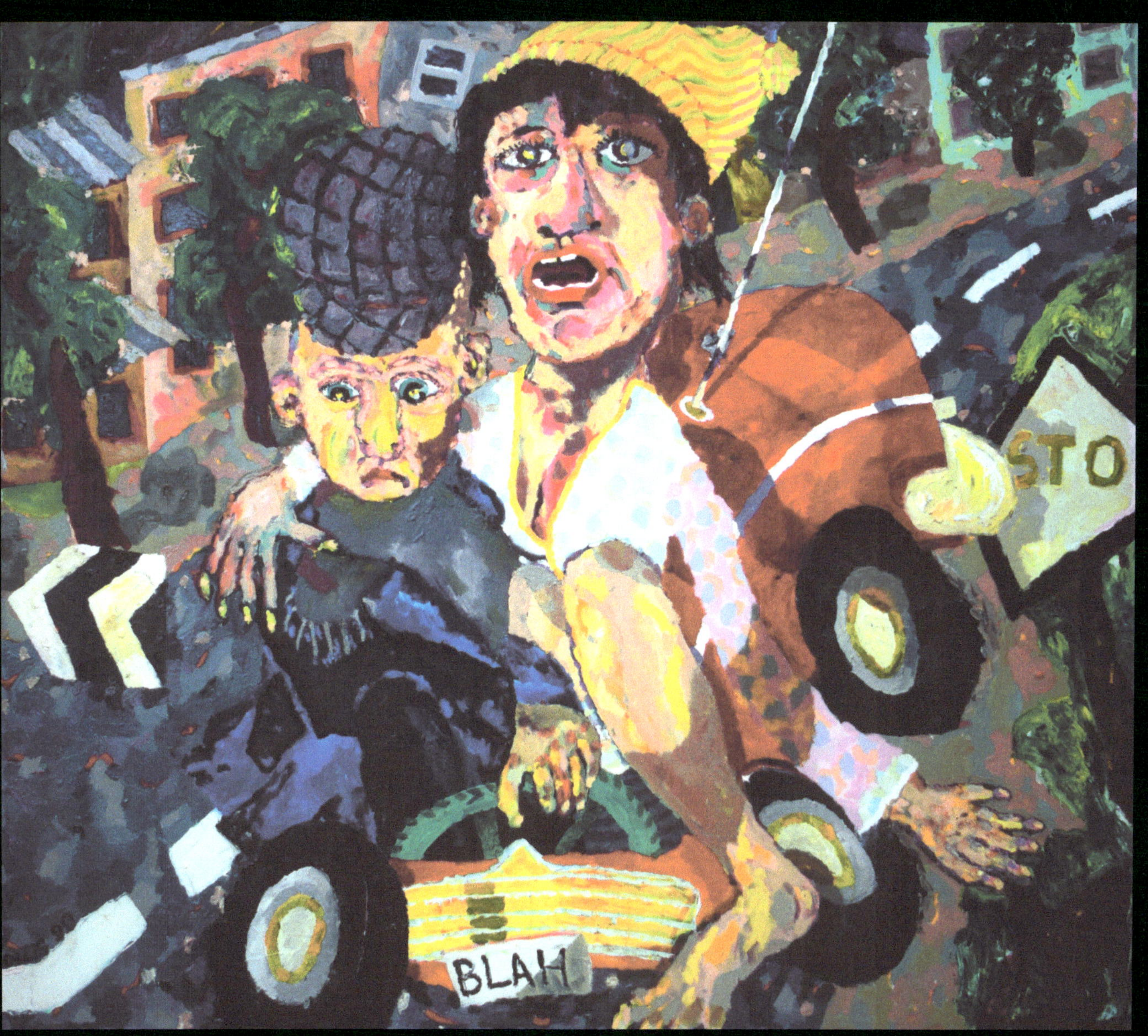

The Joyride

Oil on canvas

193 x 168cm

Collection of the Artist

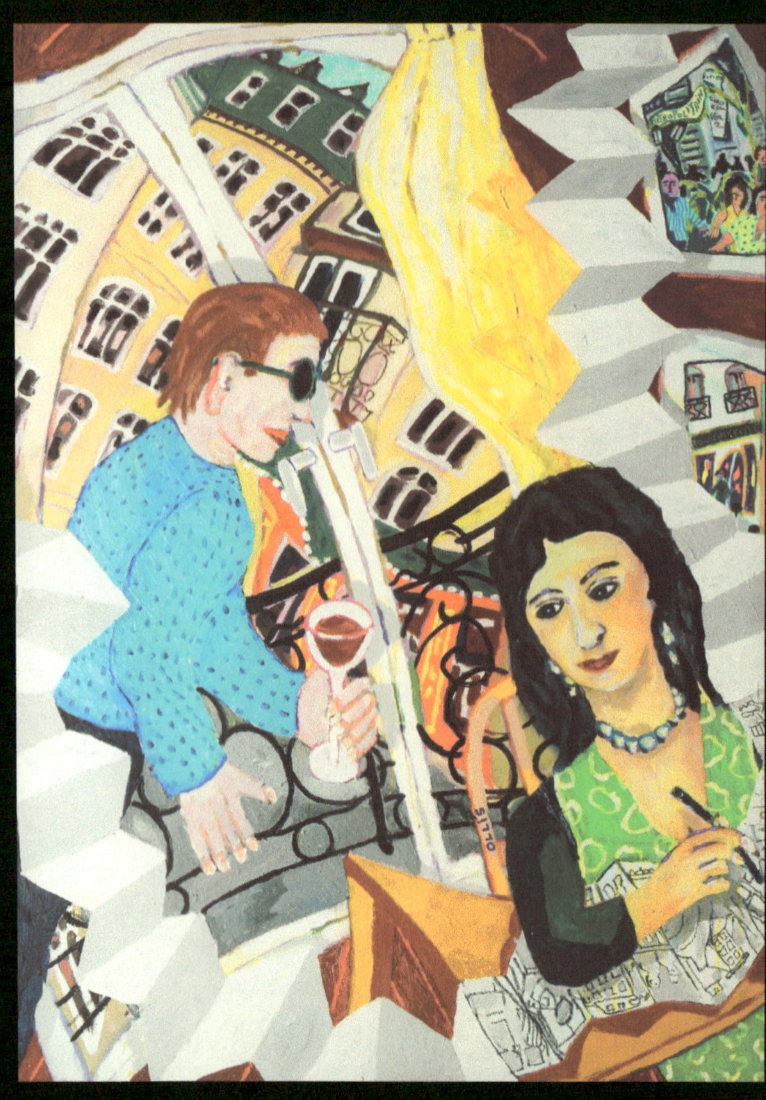

Parisian Journal

Oil on canvas

122 x 168cm

Collection of the Artist

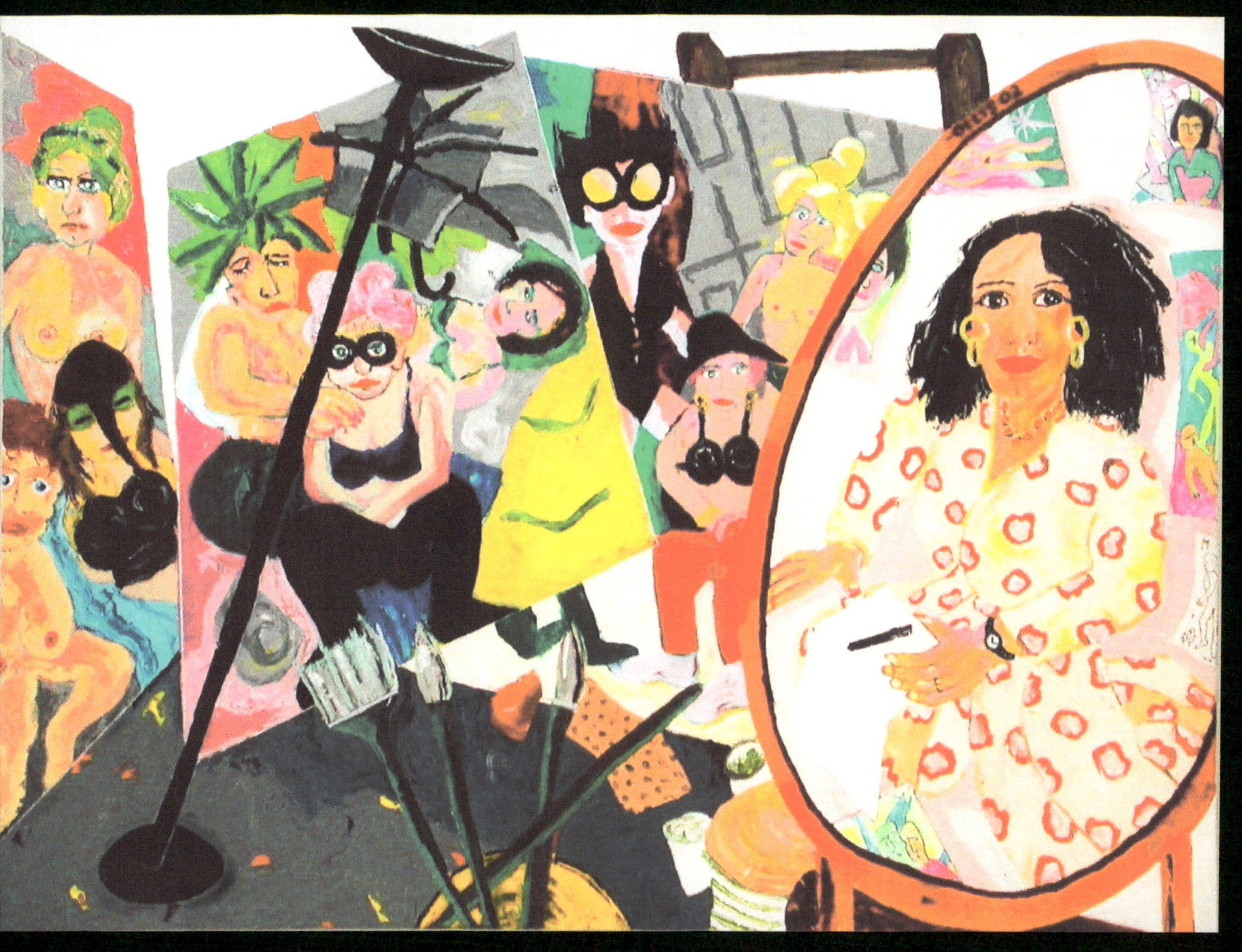

Wendy in the Studio

Oil on canvas

175 x 245cm

Collection of the Artist

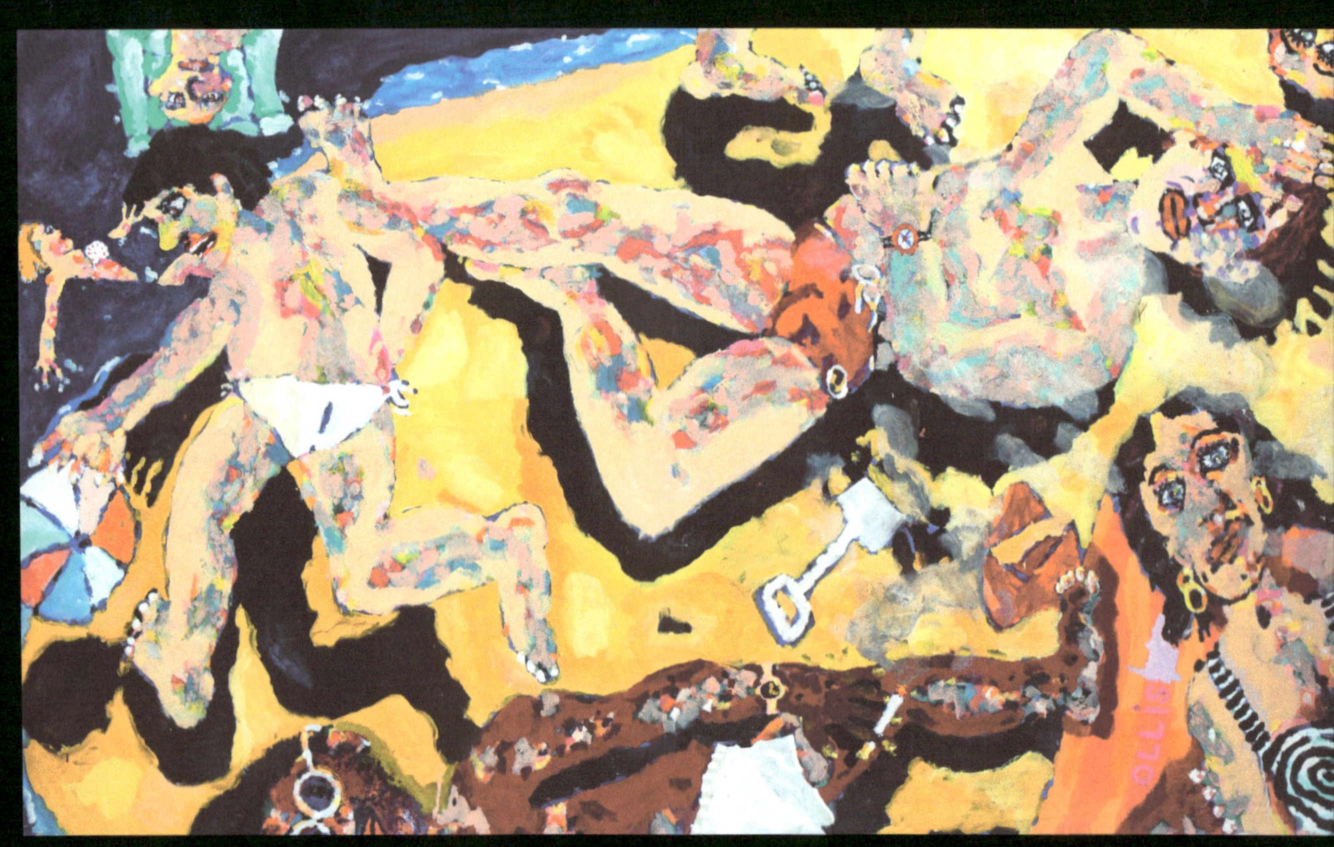

Summer Haze
Oil on canvas
170 x 283cm
Collection of the Artist

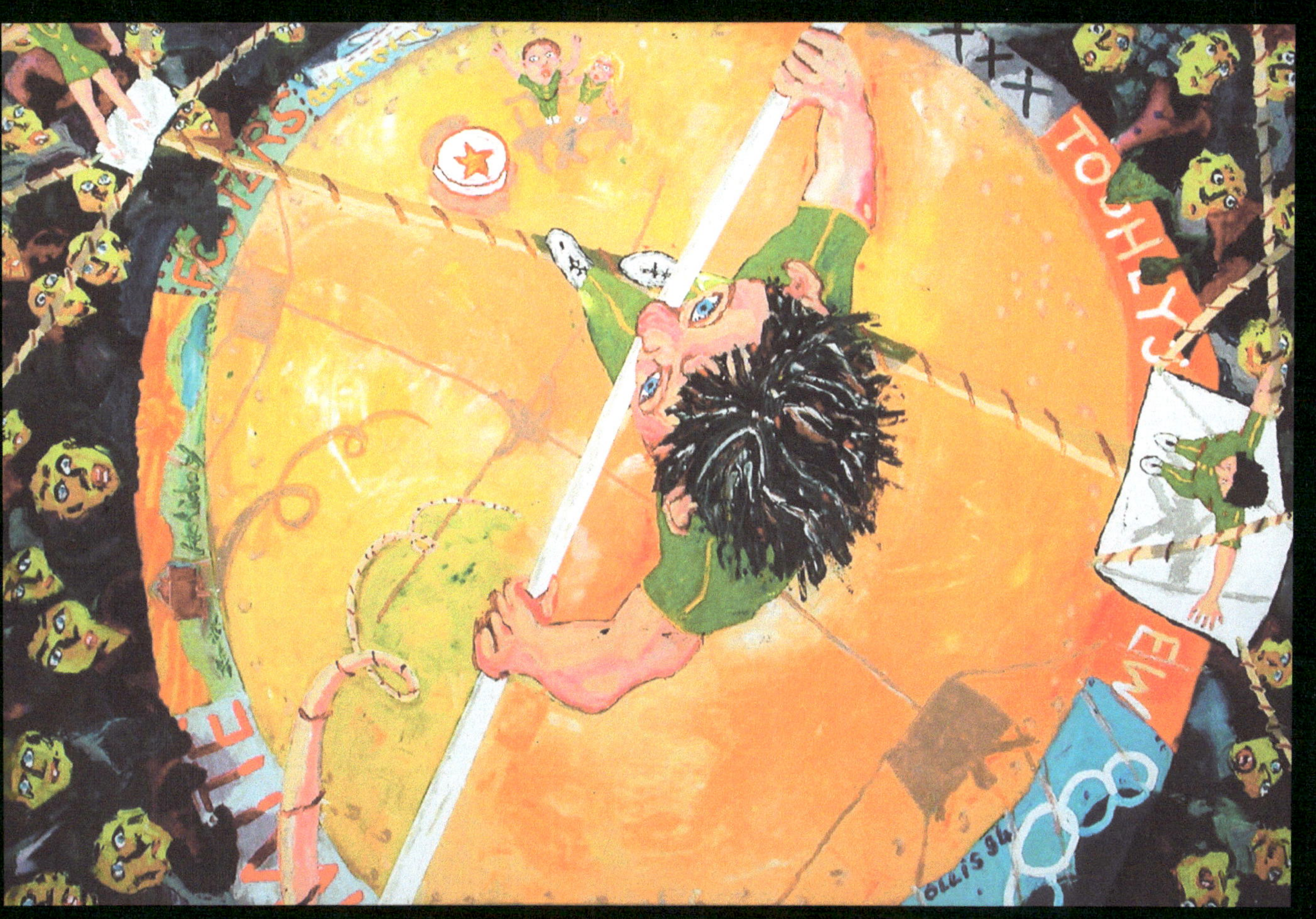

The Tightrope Walker

Oil on canvas

165 x 246cm

Collection of the Artist

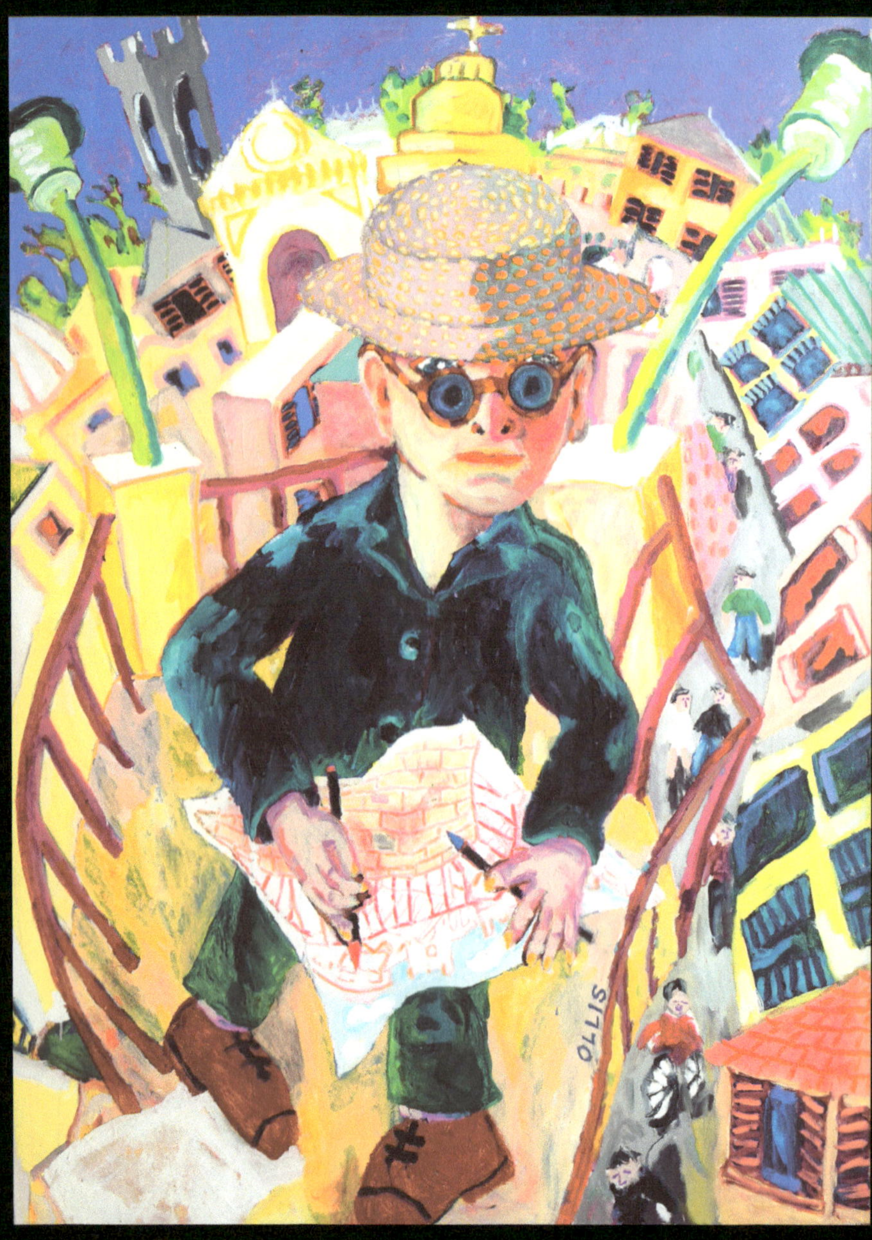

Self Portrait as an Artist in Paris

Oil on canvas

168 x 122cm

Collection of the Artist

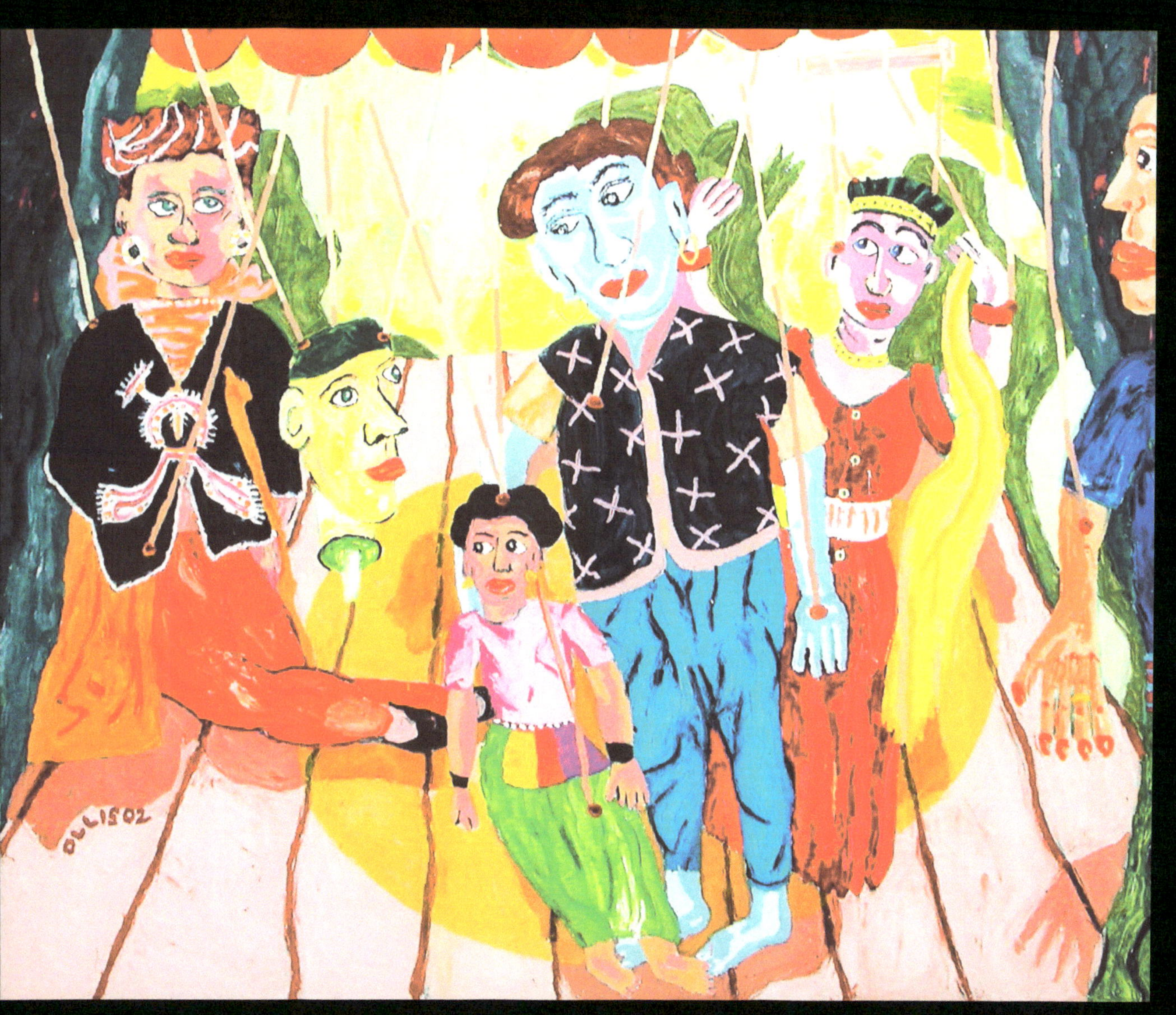

Opening Night

Oil on canvas

180 x 220cm

Collection of the Artist

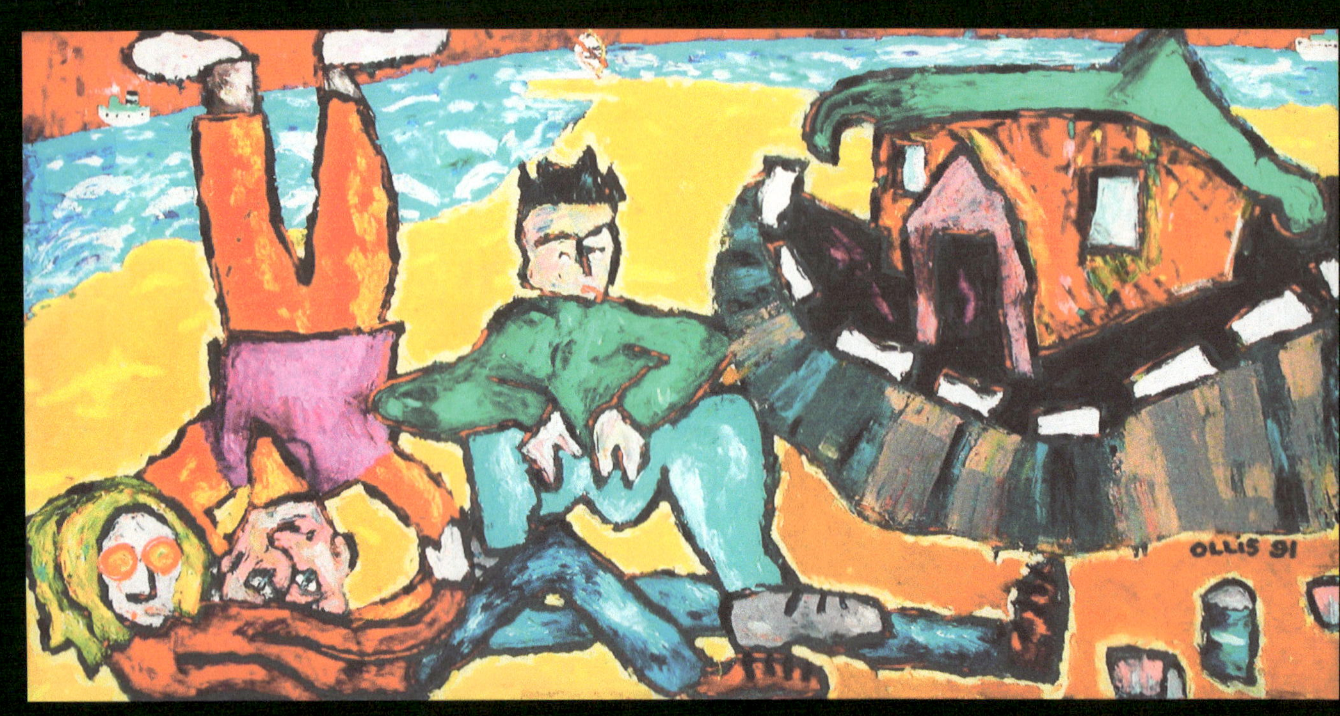

The Edge of the World

Oil on canvas

177 x 285cm
Collection of the Artist

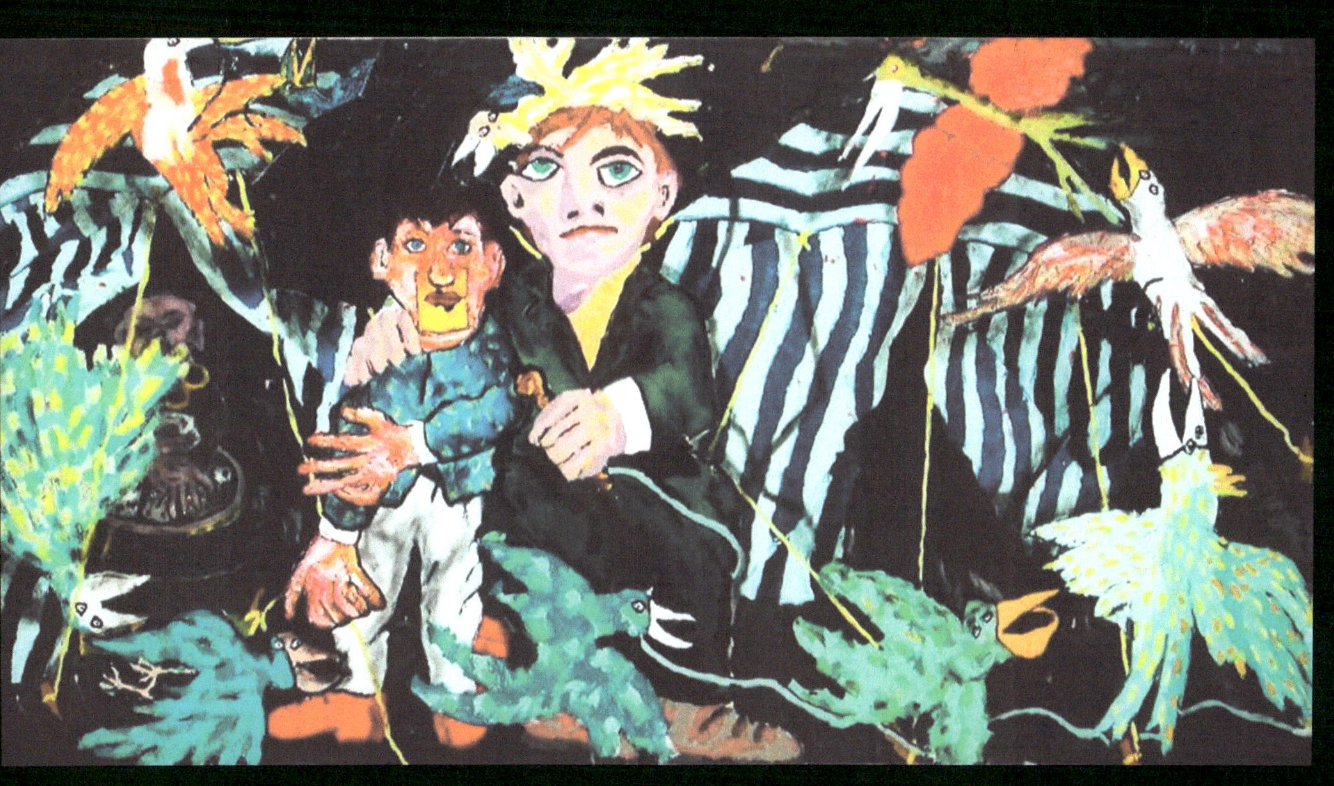

The Ventriloquist

Oil on canvas

120 x 300cm

Private collection, Perth

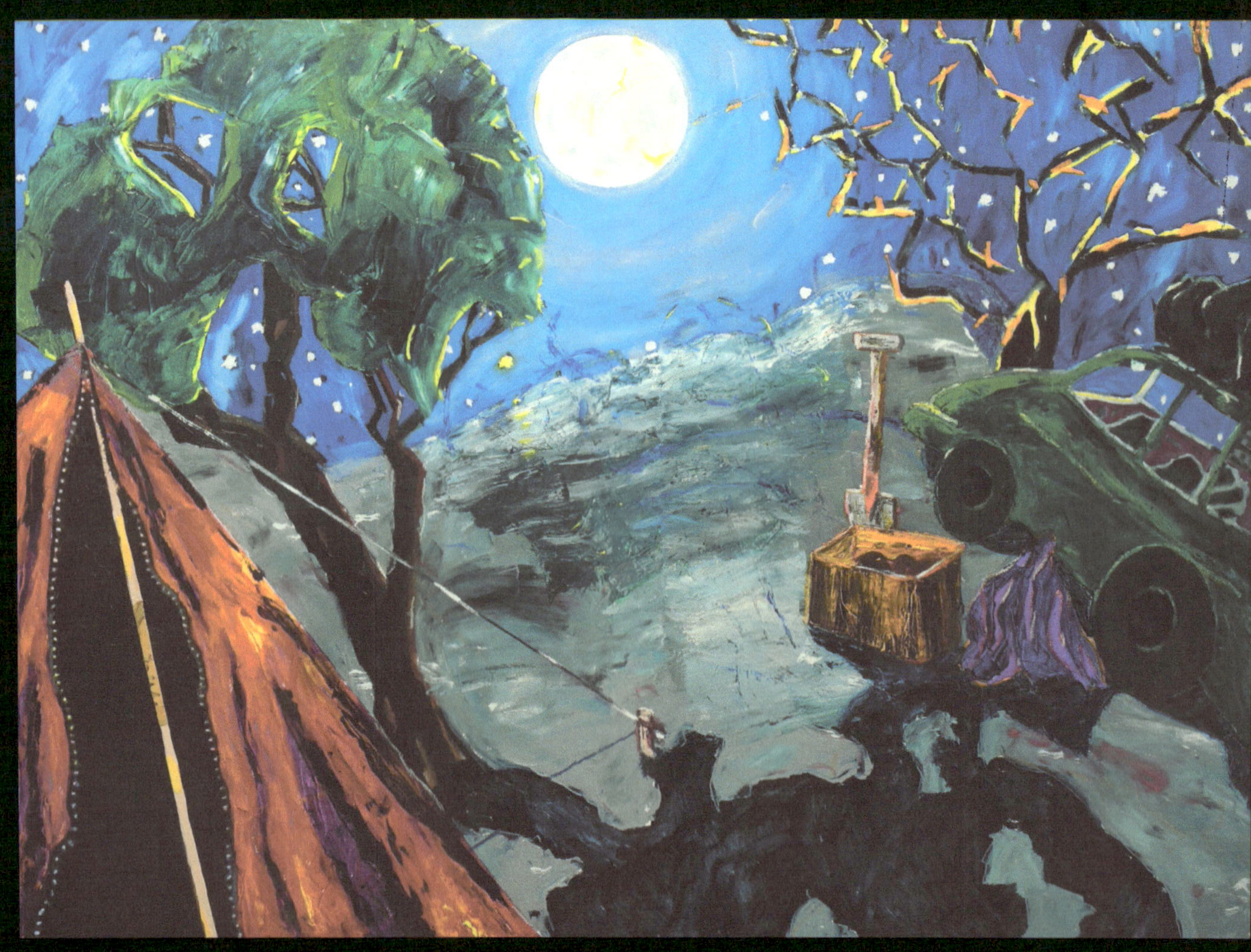

Camping Under a Full Moon

Oil on canvas

122 x 168cm
Collection of the Artist

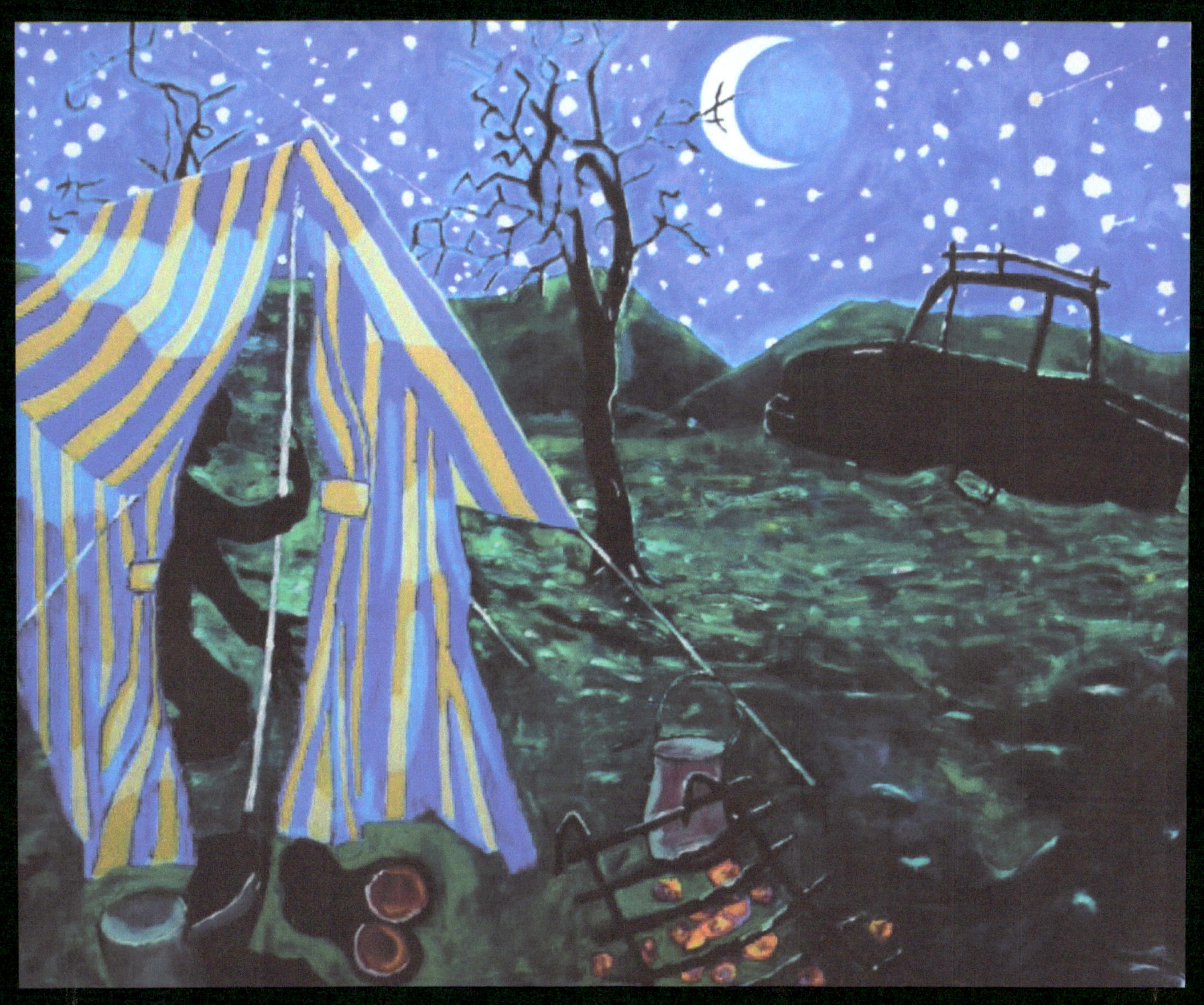

Camping Under the Stars

Oil on canvas

160 x 200cm

Private Collection, QLD

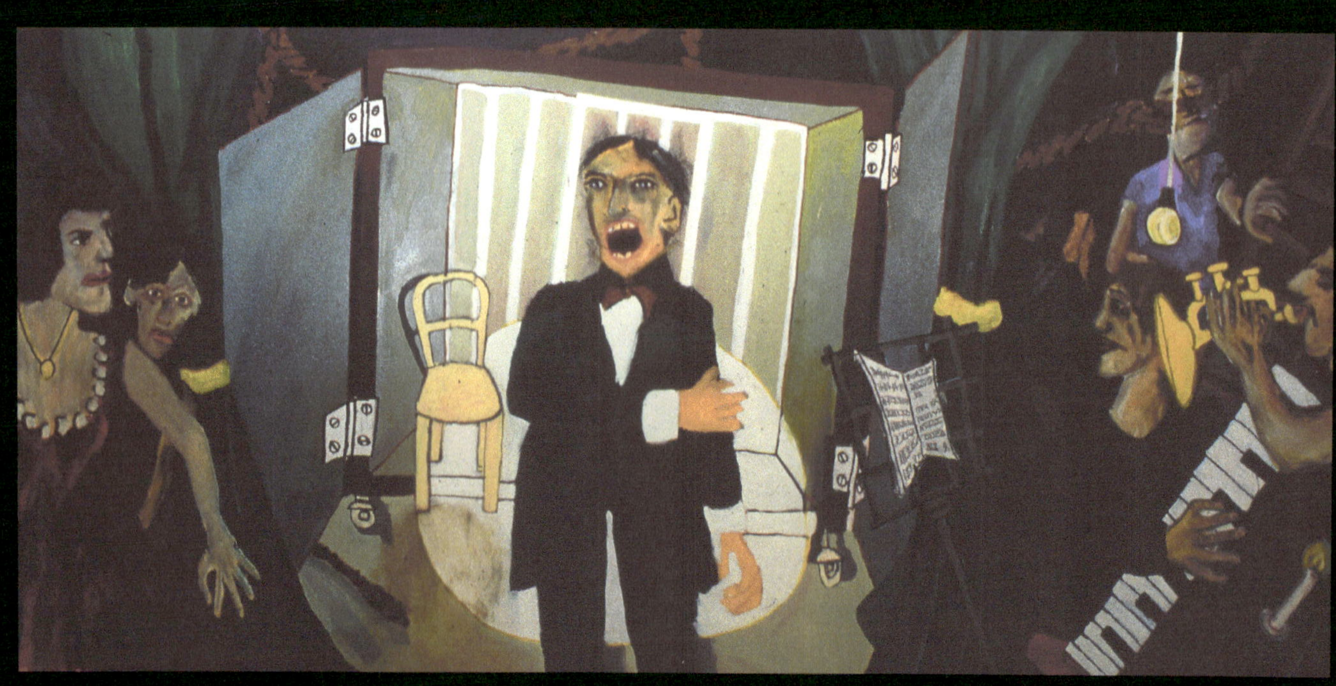

The Three Penny Opera

Oil on canvas

190 x 300cm
Private Collection, Sydney
Exhibited Macquarie Galleries Sydney 1981

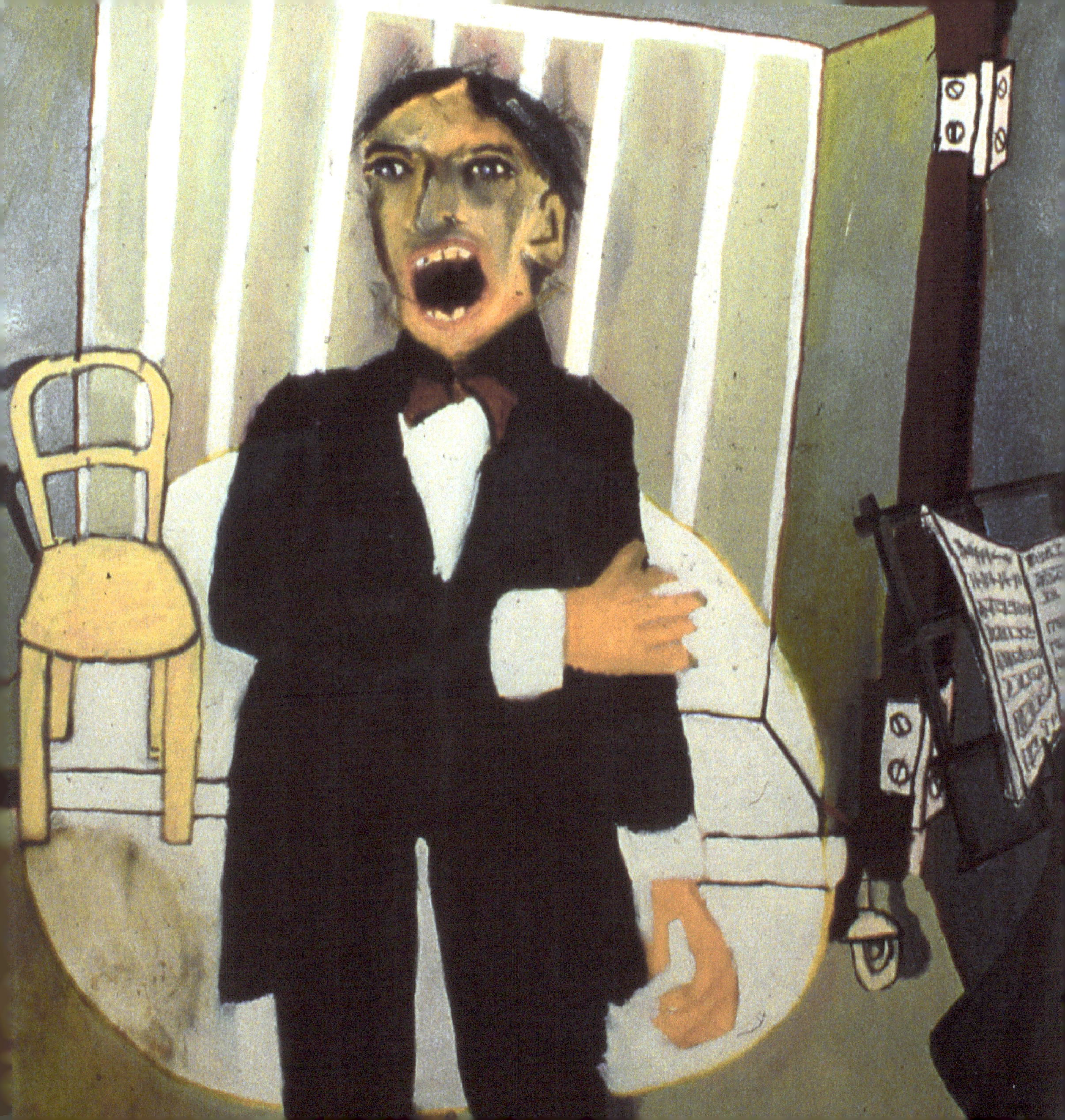

Artist Biography

Artist Biography

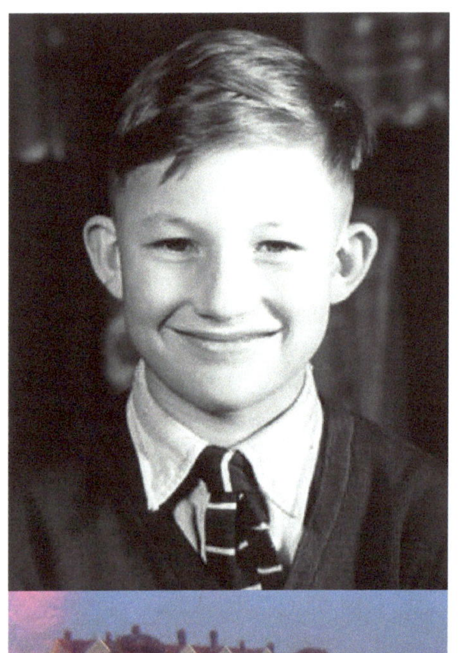
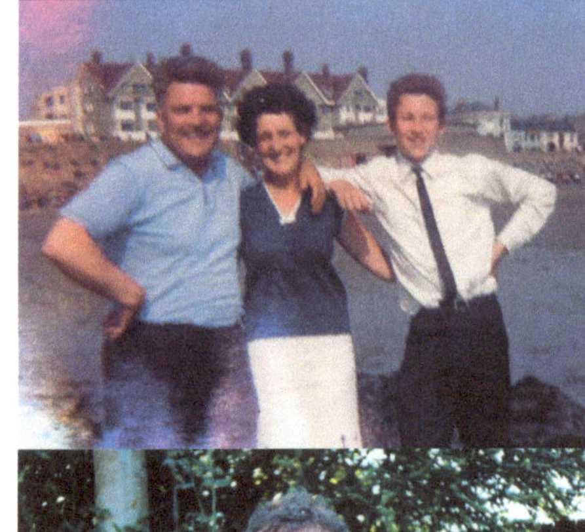
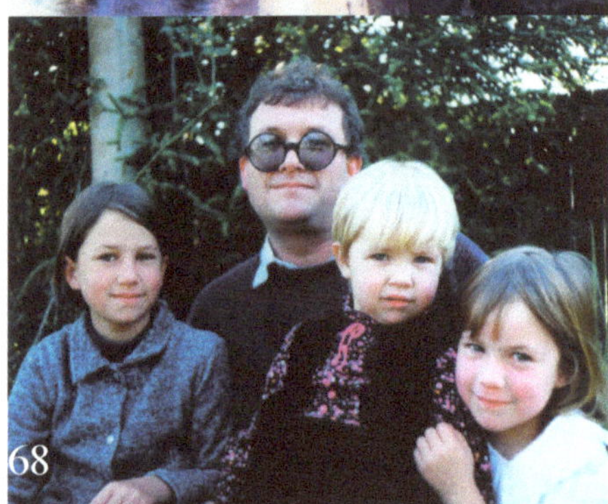

images top to bottom:
The artist, age 10 | Artist with parents on holidays in Jersey, 1965 | Artist with his three daughters Myfanwy, Madeline & Vanessa, 1982

Bernard Ollis Dip A.D. (B.A. Hons) M.A. Royal College of Art (Painting) London

1951 Born in Bath, England

1976 Arrived in Australia

Studies

1973 - 1976 Master of Art (Painting), The Royal College of Art, London UK

1970 - 1973 Diploma of Art and Design, Cardiff College of Art and Design, Wales UK

1969 - 1970 Foundation Studies Cardiff College of Art and Design, Wales UK

Lecturing and Administrative Experience

1998 – 2008 Director, National Art School (Sydney)

1997 - 1998 Head of Studies, National Art School (Sydney)

1996 - 1997 Head of Painting Department, National Art School (Sydney)

1994 - 1996 Senior Lecturer/Head of Fine Art, La Trobe University (Victoria)

1982 - 1994 Head of Painting, La Trobe University (Victoria)

1982 - Acting Head of Visual Art Department, Darwin College

1978 - 1982 Head of Painting, Drawing and Sculpture Section, Darwin College

1977 - 1978 Lecturer Fine Art, Darwin Community College

1974 - 1976 Visiting Lecturer, Various British Art Schools

Awards, Residencies and Prizes

2008 Cairo, Egypt Artist Residency, Special guest of the Australian Ambassador

2005 Conrad Jupiter Art Prize Gold Coast City Art Gallery, Queensland

2000 Olympic Arts Festival

1992 Selected by Melbourne Theatre Company for season's brochure

Awards, Residencies and Prizes (continued)

1988 Heritage Arts Festival Award, Queensland

1984 Visual Arts Board Australia, Council Grant

1983 Commissioned series of paintings for Napoleon Brandy Advertising Campaign

1982 Gold Coast City Art Awards, Queensland

1977 Sir Fredrick Richards's Travelling Scholarship (drawing), UK

1976 John Minton International Painting Prize, London UK

1975 Artist-in-residence Maltese Studio International Youth Arts Festival British representative

1975 Artist-in-residence Paris Studio Cité Internationale des Arts France

Solo Exhibitions

2011 'Major Works" Buratti Fine Art, Perth WA

2011 'Paris Revisited' NG Art Gallery, Sydney NSW

2010 'Italy' 19Karen Contemporary Artspace , Mermaid Beach, Gold Coast, Queensland

2009 'Journeys through Italy and Egypt' NG Art Gallery, Sydney NSW

2008 'Incognito' NG Art Gallery, Sydney NSW

2006 'The St Peters Suite' Michael Nagy Fine Art, Sydney NSW

2002 Stella Downer Galleries, Sydney NSW

2000 Michael Nagy Fine Art, Sydney NSW

1999 Michael Nagy Fine Art, Sydney NSW

1998 Mary Place Gallery, Sydney NSW

1998 Sydney Theatre Company, Sydney NSW

1997 Hot Bath Gallery, Bath UK

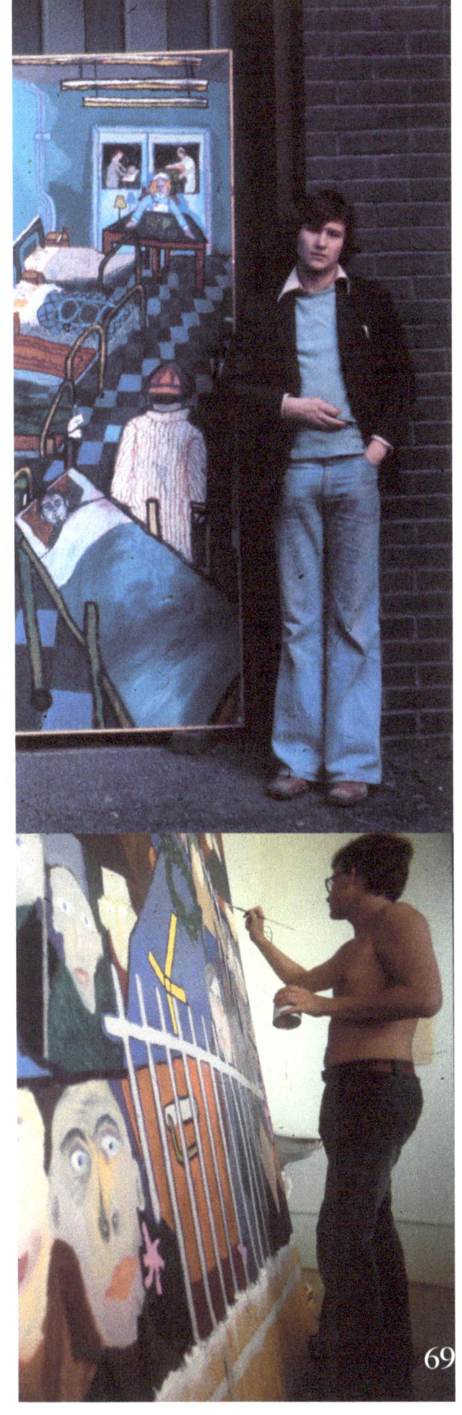

images top to bottom:
The artist studying at the Royal College of Art, London, 1975 | The artist working on canvas, Darwin, 1980

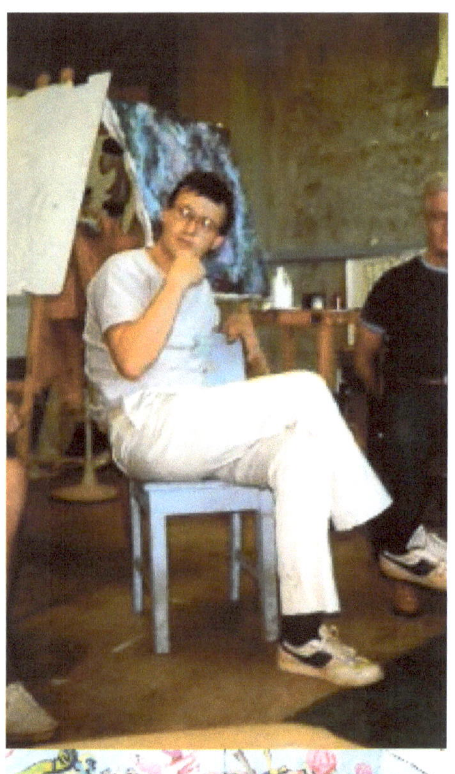

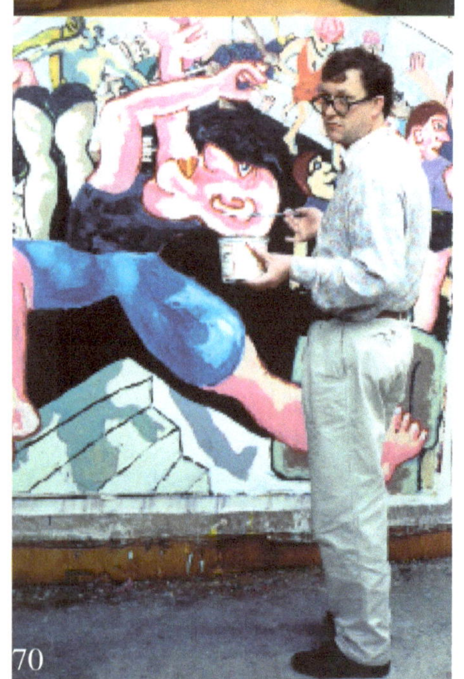

images top to bottom:
Bernard Ollis at Toowoomba, 1979 | The artist circa 1980

1993 Botanical Gallery, South Yarra Victoria

1992 Retrospective Paintings and Pastels, Macquarie Gallery, Sydney NSW

1991 Powell Street Gallery, South Yarra Victoria

1990 Macquarie Gallery, Sydney NSW

1989 Macquarie Gallery, Sydney NSW

1988 Macquarie Gallery, Sydney NSW
(also at) Roz Macallan Gallery, Brisbane Queensland

1987 Macquarie Gallery, Sydney NSW
(also at) Powell Street Gallery, South Yarra Victoria

1984 - 1986 Visual Arts Board, 'Bernard Ollis' The Australian Tour
(exhibited at)
Undercroft Gallery for the Perth Festival University of Western Australia
Hawthorn City Art Gallery, Victoria
Warrnambool Art Gallery, Victoria
Ararat Gallery, Victoria
Mildura Arts Centre, Victoria
Shepparton Regional Art Gallery, Victoria
Muswellbrook Art Gallery, NSW
Bathurst Regional Gallery, NSW
Orange Art Gallery, NSW
Benalla Art Gallery Victoria
Wagga Wagga Art Gallery, NSW
Bendigo Art Gallery Victoria (extended survey exhibition)

1984 Macquarie Gallery, Sydney NSW

1982 Macquarie Gallery, Sydney NSW

1981 Macquarie Gallery, Sydney NSW

1978 Warehouse Galleries, South Melbourne Victoria

1976 The Africa Centre Covent Garden, London UK

1976 The Royal Commonwealth Society, London UK

1974 - 1975 Commonwealth Institute Gallery, London UK

1972 - 1973 College of Art Gallery, Cardiff Wales

Selected Group Exhibitions

2009 "The Grand Tour" United Galleries, Perth WA

2009 "Every Dog has his Day" Letham Gallery, Aukland, NZ

2009 "Ceramic Platters" Delmar Gallery, Sydney

2008 "Urban Myth" (2 person show with Wendy Sharp) United Galleries, Perth

2008 "Contemporary Drawing" Wimbledon Art College Gallery, London, UK

2006 Hong Ik University Gallery, Seoul, South Korea

2005 "Drawcard" Cell Block Theatre, NAS, Sydney

2005 "Dog Trumpet" Michael Nagy Gallery, Sydney

2005 "Drawing the line" Cell Block Theatre, NAS, Sydney

2004 "Drawcard" Cell Block Theatre, NAS, Sydney

2004 Hong Ik University gallery, Seoul, South Korea

2004 Doug Moran Portrait Prize, Finalist, Mitchell Library (Touring Australia)

2004 "Spectrum" NSW Parliament House, FONAS Exhibition

2003 Dobell Prize, Finalist, Art Gallery of New South Wales

2003 "Beneath the Surface" Cell Block Theatre, NAS, Sydney

2002 Sulman Prize, Finalist, Art Gallery of New South Wales

2001 The Studio Tradition, Finalist (Touring), Manly Art Gallery

2001 Sulman Prize, Finalist, Art Gallery of New South Wales

2000 Sulman Prize, Finalist, Art Gallery of New South Wales

2000 Olympic Arts Festival Sydney (Various Locations)

1998 Pas D'Accrochage En Publique (Not a Public Hanging) National Art School

1997 Dominique Segan Drawing Prize, Castlemaine, Victoria

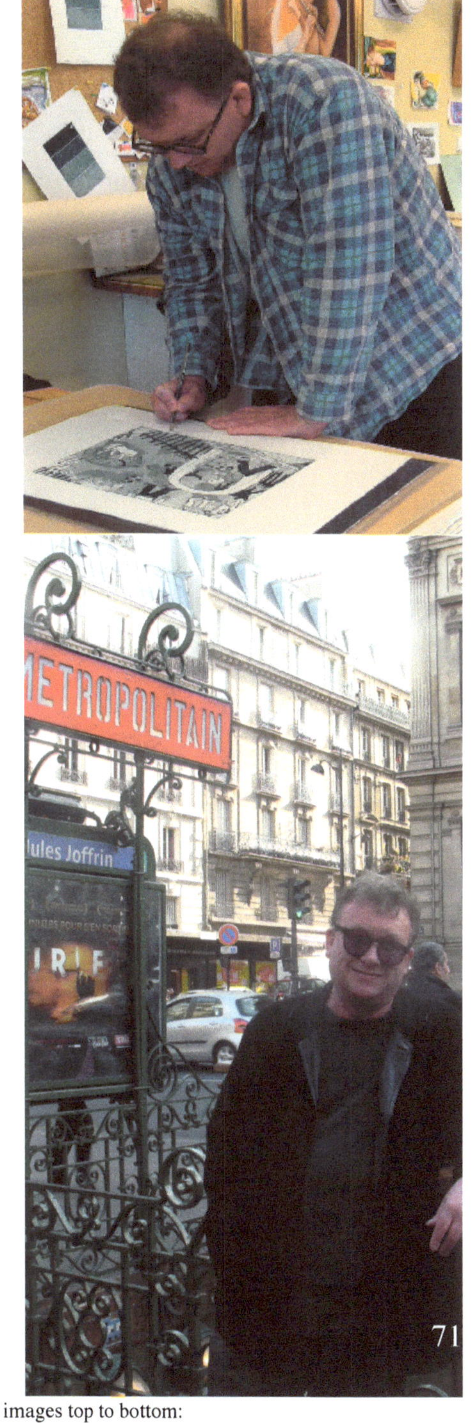

images top to bottom:
Bernard Ollis signing prints at Falls Gallery NSW |
The artist at the Jules Joffrin Metro station near his Paris studio 2010 |

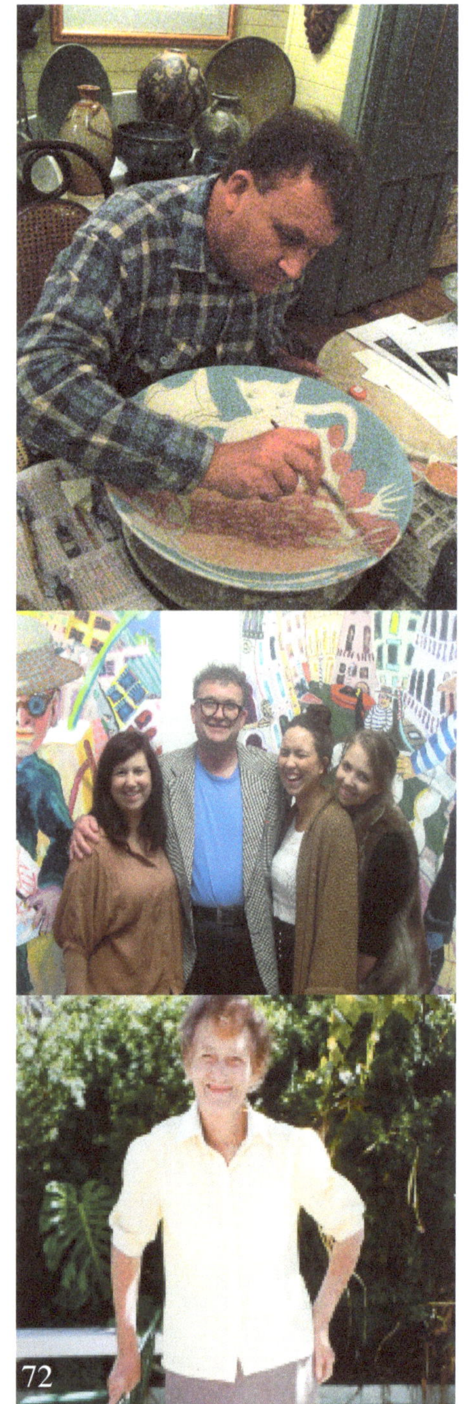

images top to bottom:
The artist working on ceramics | Artist in studio with his three daughters Myfanwy, Madeline and Vanessa 2011 | The artist's mother visiting Australia

1995 - 1996 "Sport, The Most Accessible Theatre in the World"

1995 Australia Felix Benalla Easter Arts Festival, Victoria

1995 "The Mask" Amnesty International, Art Gallery of New South Wales

1995 "The Comedie Humane" Co-curated Australian Galleries, Sydney

1994 La Trobe University, Bundoora Victoria (staff exhibition)

1994 QDOS Gallery, Lorne Victoria

1992 Summer School Tutors Downs Gallery, University of Southern Queensland

1992 "Artists Play" Westpac Gallery, Melbourne Victoria

1991 Solander Gallery, Canberra ACT

1991 Art Space, Bendigo Victoria

1991 Lake Macquarie Invitation Prize University Gallery, Sydney

1990 Solander Gallery, Canberra ACT

1990 Art Space, Bendigo Victoria

1990 Lake Macquarie Invitation Prize University Gallery, Sydney

1989 Fremantle International Print Award Exhibition, Fremantle Gallery WA

1989 University of New South Wales Purchase Prize, University Gallery Sydney

1989 Art Space, Bendigo Victoria

1989 Lake Macquarie Invitation Prize, University Gallery Sydney NSW

1988 9" x 5" Centenary Exhibition touring NSW and QLD regional Galleries

1988 Art Space, Bendigo Victoria

1987 University of New South Wales Purchase Prize, University Gallery Sydney

1987 Art Space, Bendigo Victoria

1986 Solander Gallery, Canberra ACT

1983 Anima Galleries, Adelaide SA

1982 Macquarie Galleries, Sydney NSW

1982 "Urban Environment" Travelling Exhibition, Ivan Dougherty Gallery Sydney and Regional Galleries of New South Wales

1981 Contemporary Arts Society, Adelaide SA

1980 College Gallery Darwin Community College, Darwin NT

1980 Browns Mart Theatre Company, Darwin NT

1978 Museum and Art Gallery of the Northern Territory, Darwin NT

1977 "Work on Paper" Macquarie Galleries, Sydney NSW

1976 The Royal College of Art Gulbenkian Hall, London UK

1975 "New Contemporaries of British Art" Camden Arts Centre, London UK

1975"Northern Young Contemporaries", Manchester UK

1974 Commonwealth Institute Arts Centre, London UK

1973 Brunel University with David Hockney, Peter Blake and Ron Kitaj, London UK

1970 Welsh Arts Council (acquisitive), Cardiff Wales

1970 Stowels Trophy Award - Institute of Contemporary Art, London, UK

Collections (Works acquired by galleries & institutions)

Art Bank, Sydney, NSW

Australian National Gallery, Canberra, ACT

Ballarat Art Gallery and Museum, Ballarat, Victoria

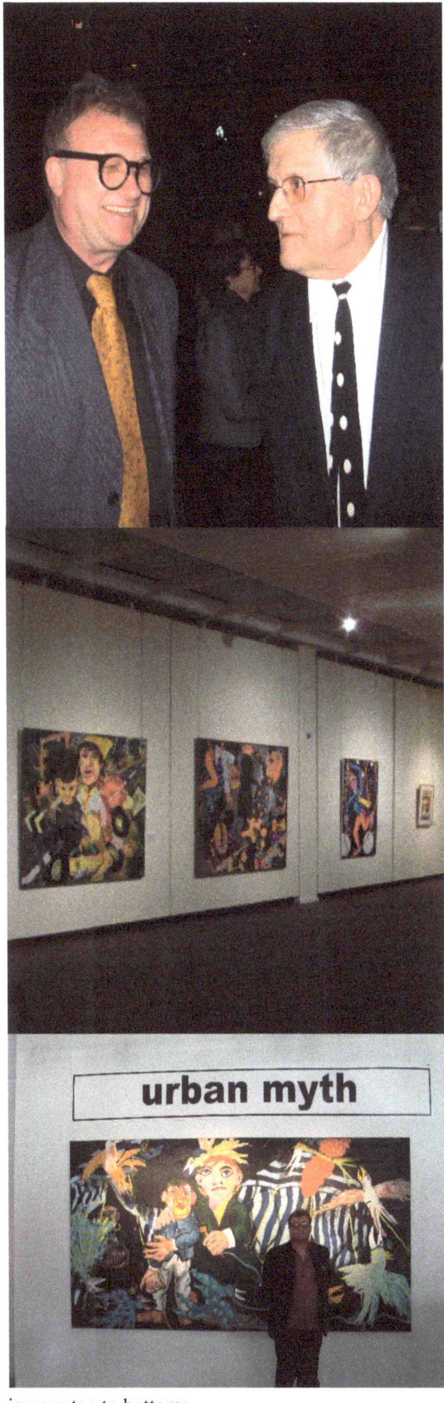

images top to bottom:
The artist with David Hockney, Paris 2010 | Installation of Bernard Ollis works at the Orange Regional Gallery NSW 2010 | The artist in Perth, 2008

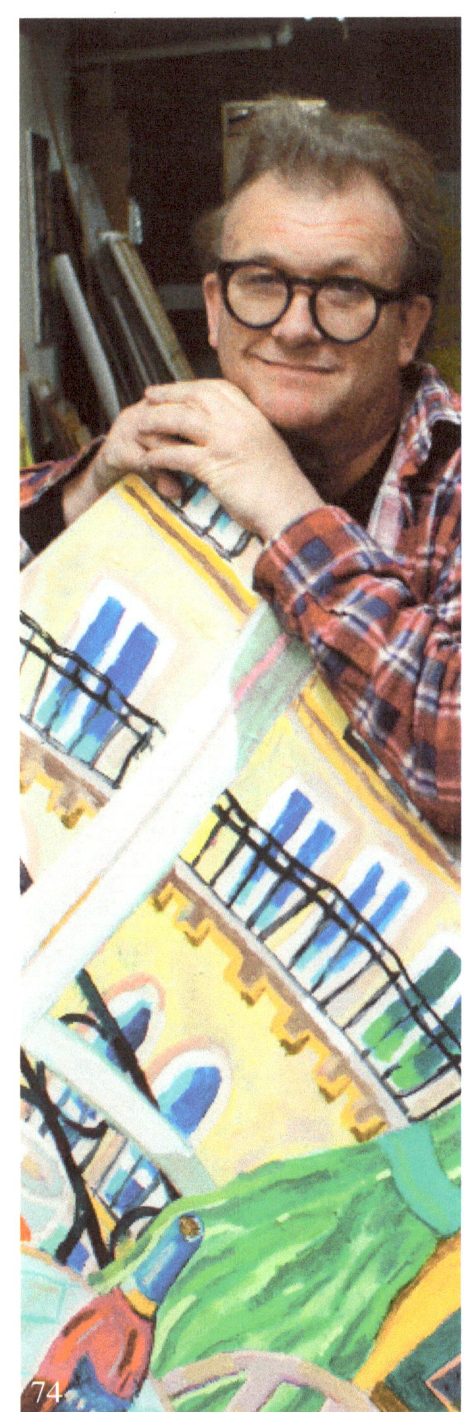

left: the artist in the studio, 2011
right: Bernard Ollis and Wendy Sharpe sketching in Varanesi India | St Peters Studio | The artist at home, 2008

Gold Coast City Art Gallery, Surfers Paradise, Queensland

Grafton Regional Gallery, Grafton, NSW

Herald Sun Art Collection, Melbourne, Victoria

La Trobe University, Melbourne, Victoria

McGregor Collection University of Southern Queensland, Toowoomba, Queensland

Museum and Art Gallery of the Northern Territory

National Gallery of Victoria, Melbourne, Victoria

New England Regional Art Museum, Armidale, NSW

Orange Regional Art Gallery, Orange, NSW

Parliament House, Canberra, ACT

Queensland Art Gallery, Brisbane, Queensland

Royal College of Art, London, UK

Royal Melbourne Institute of Technology, Victoria

The Commonwealth Institute, London, UK

Welsh Arts Council, Cardiff, Wales, UK

Selected reviews

2011 Buratti, Robert, Artist Profile, October

2006 McDonald, John, Australian Art Collector

2005 Hill, Peter, Line Honours, Sydney Morning Herald, 4 September

2004 Verghis, Sharon, Art teacher draws a line at new skills, Sydney Morning Herald, 12 June

1998 Morgan, Joyce, New Era as Disharmony goes by the Board, Sydney Morning Herald, 11 February

1995 The Power of Ten, Herald Sun, April

1991 Image: The Body Swap Shop, Bathurst Regional Gallery

1991 Robert, Rooney, No Rest for the Wicked, Weekend Australian, February

1990 Chanin, Eileen, Inside World, Macquarie Gallery Bulletin

1989 Farrel, Katrina, Jumping in the Deep End, Australian Arts

1988 Catalano, Gary, A Review of the Year in the Galleries, The Age, December

1988 Chanin, Eileen, New Art 11, Macquarie Gallery Bulletin

1988 Catalano, Gary, Fantasy Moves Out of the Fairground, The Age, 17 February

1988 Constantine, Fran, 9 x 5 x Mail The Centre Gallery, Queensland

1986 Malcolm, Terrance, How to Handle Child?s Play, Sydney Morning Herald,

1986 Black, Sharyn, Ollis Rocking the Boat, BCAE Student Magazine

1985 Catalano, Gary, Australian Ugliness as seen by English Eyes, The Age, June

1985 Chanin, Eileen, and Ollis, Bernard, Constructivism, Macquarie Galleries Bulletin

1984 Tobias, Jill, Bendigo Artist's Work Home to Roost, Bendigo Advertiser, September

1984 McGrath, Sandra, Place Conveyed as State of Mind, The Weekend Australian,

1984 The Bulletin, 24 July

1984 Wolseley, John, Bonjour Monsieur Ollis, Macquarie Gallery, Bulletin

1983 Artworks go on Show, Mildura Paper

1983 Art is Vibrant and Colourful, Mildura Paper

1983 Art on Show, Mildura Paper

1983 At the Gallery, The News, Shepparton, 15 September

1981 Borlase, Nancy, It all there the Beer, the View and the Colour, Sydney Morning Herald

1981 A Month in Review, National Times, August

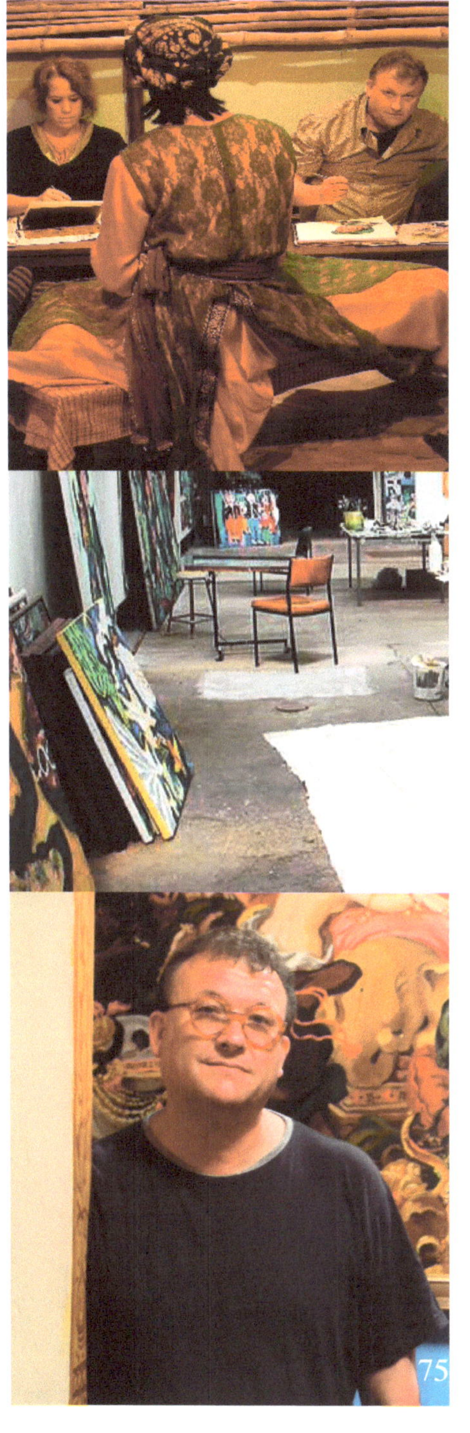

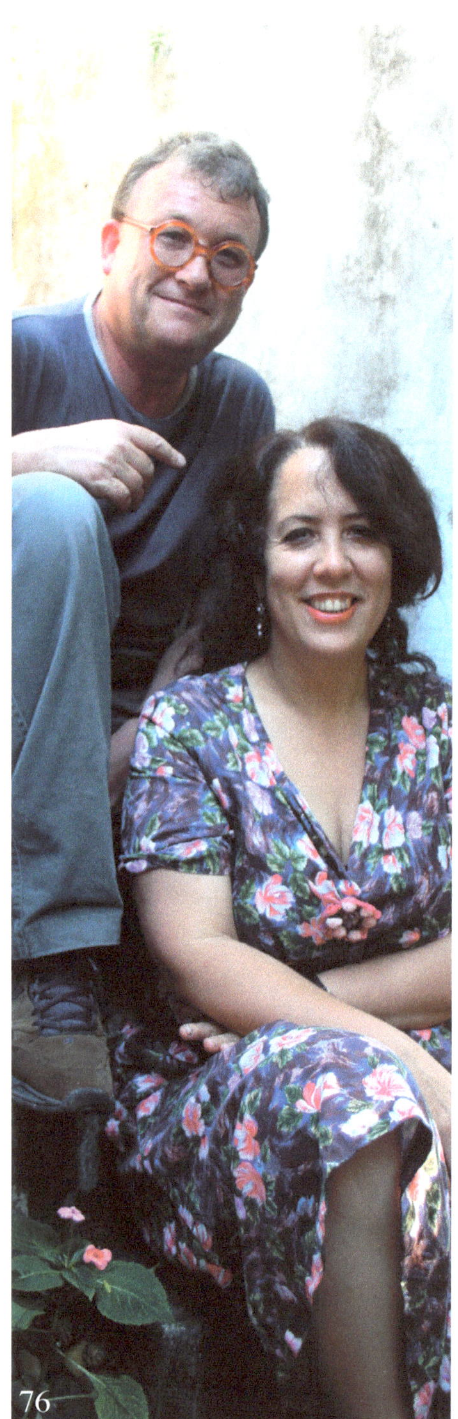

left: The artist with partner, Wendy Sharpe 2008
right: The artist in his studio, Paris France 2010

Catalogues and Books

2011 Robert Buratti, The Art of Bernard Ollis, Buratti Fine Art

2006 McCulloch, Alan, McCulloch's Encycopedia of Australian Art, (4th edition) Aus Art Editions/The Miegunyah Press Victoria ISBN 0 522 85317 X

2006 Ollis, Bernard, The St Peters Suite, ISBN 0 646 46173 7

2005 Li Jingzhe, Australian Contemporary Painting Shanghai Peoples Fine Art Publishing House

1997 Paterson, Susan, From Bendigo to Bath, Hot Bath Gallery, Bath, UK

1996 Paterson, S. and Gervasoni, C. Catbuster Studio Art, Macmillan, Victoria

1995 Who?s Who of Australian Visual Arts (2nd edition) Reed International Publishing

1995 Gervasoni, Clare, and Paterson, Susan, Catbuster Art, Macmillan, Melbourne

1994 McCulloch, Susan, The Encyclopaedia of Australian Art, Allen and Unwin, Melbourne

1993 Hayes, Susan, and Gervasoni, Clare, Artistic Insights, Harcourt Brace Jovanonvich, Sydney

1992 Drury, Neville, Images in Contemporary Art, Craftsman House, Sydney

1991 Chanin, Eileen, ed Contemporary Australian Art, Craftsman House, Sydney

1990 Germaine, Max, Artists and Galleries of Australia, Craftsman House, Sydney

1988 Drury, Neville, New Directions in Contemporary Art, Craftsman House, Sydney

1984 Bendigo Art Gallery Bernard Ollis Australian Works, National Touring catalogue

1983 Paroissien, Leon, Australian Art Review, Warner Assoc. Press

Contributions to Books, Journals and Magazines by Bernard Ollis

2005 Ollis, Bernard, the Band Returning 2005 full page colour image appearing on the front cover of Antiques & Art in Queensland November 2005 March 2006 edi-

1998 Ollis, Bernard, History of the National Art School, NAS website

1992 Ollis, Bernard, in Hayes, Susan, Flora and Fauna, La Trobe University

1983 Ollis, Bernard, An Artists view from Darwin, Australian Art Review Chapter on
Northern Territory. Ed Paroissien, Leon, Macmillan Press

1980 Ollis, Bernard, catalogue preface introduction to David Middlebrook American
Artist in Residence, Chandler Coventry Gallery

1980 Ollis, Bernard, Peter Colett, in Scarlett Ken Australian Sculptors, Nelson, Melbourne

1976 Ollis, Bernard, chapter in Picard Phyllis If You think Your Child is Gifted,
Allen and Unwin, London

1975 Ollis, Bernard, Malta seminars become Carnivals Commonwealth News 4 June 75

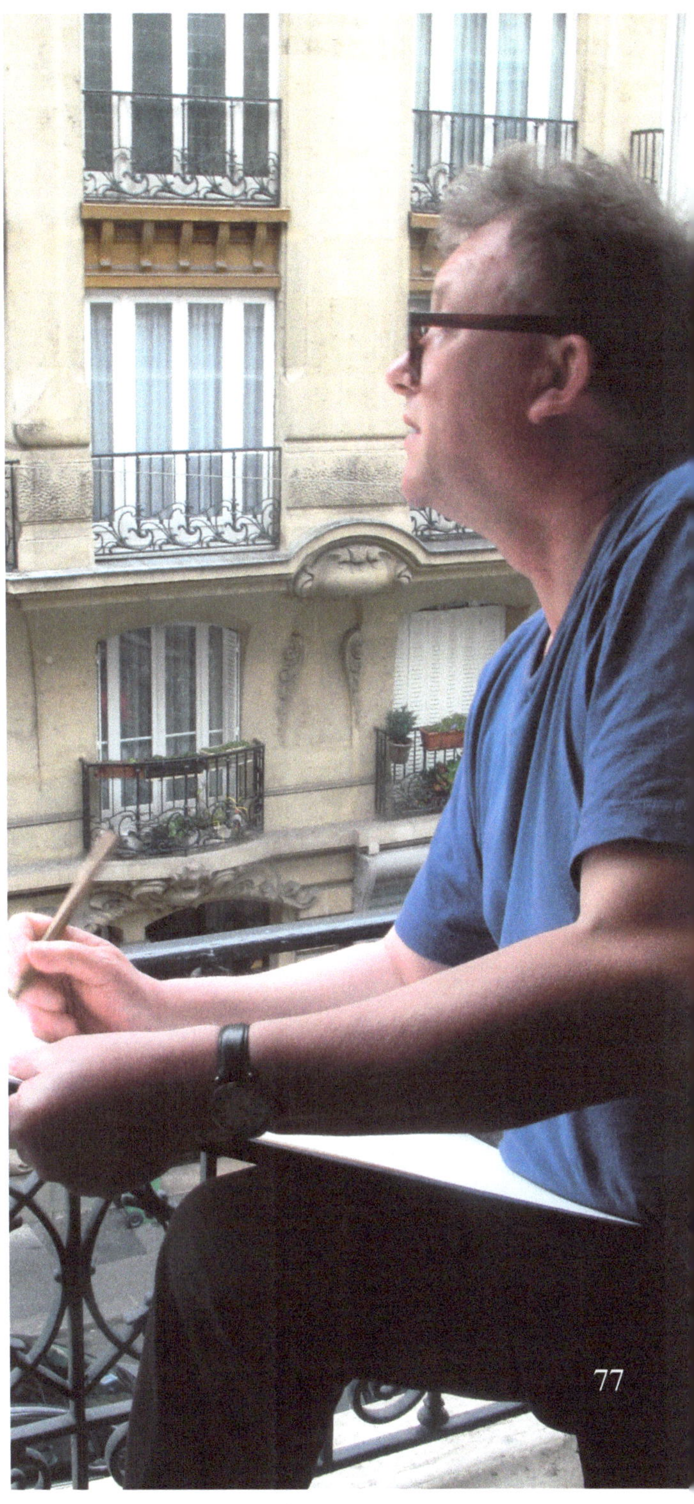

BURATTI

FINE ART

www.ingramcontent.com/pod-product-compliance
Lightning Source LLC
LaVergne TN
LVHW070508120826
845147LV00031BA/265
* 9 7 8 0 9 8 7 2 0 7 8 1 4 *